# Mickie's Diaries
# 1926 to 1940

# Table of Contents

# Introduction

———◦◇◦———

I am the daughter of Elinor Mary Wheeler Nichols. My mother and her twin sister, Elizabeth Louise Wheeler, were born in 1910 and were dancers known as "The Wheeler Twins". They danced professionally from 1927 until 1935 when my mother's twin broke her back doing a curtain call on stage.

This book will include the most interesting events of my mother's diaries and I do hope my family and friends enjoy it. I have also taken the liberty to insert photos throughout this book of the Wheeler Twins dancing, as well as places and events that touched their lives.

I wish to dedicate this book to my son, Robby, who was with me every step of the way as we read together and decided which passages should be included to make this book of my mother's career.

The Wheeler twins at age 2. (1912)

Elinor Wheeler

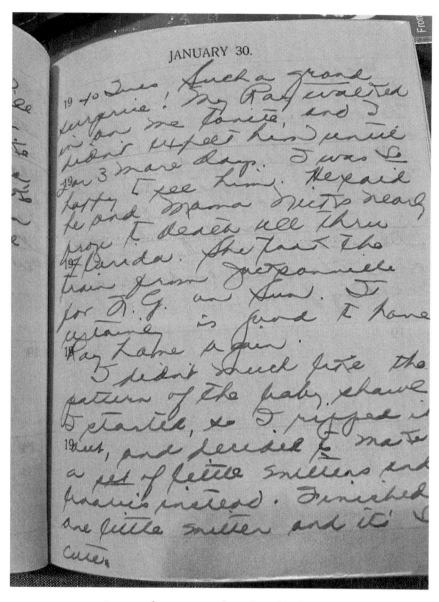

A page from one of twelve diaries.....

Original diaries from 1926 through 1940.

Mickie's Diaries 1926 to 1940

# Mickie's Diaries 1926 – 1940

———◆◇◆———

Mickie's Diaries....A Vaudeville Dancer's Career....in her own words....

EDITOR'S NOTE:

The Wheeler Twins, Elinor Mary and Elizabeth Louise, were born April 21, 1910, to Harry Beech Wheeler and Wilna Mary English Wheeler (age 22) in Indianapolis, Indiana.

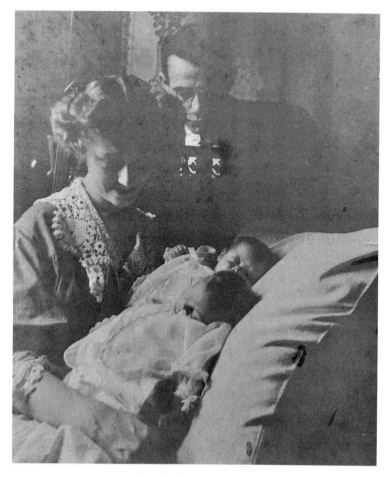

Newborn twins.......

Nearly 1 year old in their pram....

With their mother, 2 1/2 years old.

Elinor and Elizabeth at age 8 with their parents.

EDITOR'S NOTE:

The first diary starts in 1926 when Mickie (Elinor) and Betty (Elizabeth) were 16 years old. The following are journal entries taken from 12 years of diaries written by Elinor beginning during their teen years and getting into and then starring in Vaudeville, Broadway, and on the S.S.Paris cruise liner and at the London Palladium.

1926. Elinor, mother Wilna, Elizabeth.

But first, diary entries by my mother, Elinor Wheeler, at age 16, as she experienced a horrific hurricane with her mother and twin sister...in her own words....

HURRICANE OF 1926........,Miami Beach, Florida, September 19, 1926. During the day, a hurricane was predicted, but we thought nothing of it until about 11 PM when it began to blow pretty hard. Betts and I went to bed on the sleeping porch and Mother decided to stay up longer to see what would happen. By 12 midnight it began to blow hard, so Betty went in and began to read with Mother, but I was sound asleep, so I knew nothing about it. For three weeks previous to this, I had been very ill with abscess in my ears and at the same time was suffering so with the pain that the doctor had to give me morphine to keep me asleep and ease the intense suffering.

About 1 AM the lights went out and Mother lit three little candles that she found and by 1:30 AM the wind had increased very very much. She woke me and made me come inside so she could close the doors of the sleeping porch. Our apartment faced the ocean on Ocean Drive and the porch looked right out on the ocean, so we got the full force of the wind. About 4:15 AM Mother decided we were really in for something very serious, so she stripped the bed of mattresses and bedding on the porch and got the doors closed again just as the rains came down in solid sheets of water. Then she got us to dress and go into the dining room and eat bread and jelly and run the Victrola, which sounds silly now I guess, but it seemed the sensible thing to do then.

Mother thought she would make as much fun of it as she could, so she stuck some white rubber (waterproof) flowers in her hair as being appropriate for a wet evening and pretty soon we were in gales of laughter. I'd even forgotten the pain in my ears!

Just then Paul Evans, a peach of a man we knew, burst in the door. He had been knocking, but the noise of the strong wind and water was so terrible, we could not hear him, so he jerked the catch off the door. He expected to come in and find us all hysterical with fear, and there we were as cool as cucumbers. Meanwhile, water was coming in around all the windows, the sleeping porch was a complete wreck minus every awning and screens and curtains, and everything else. The candles were long since gone so we all decided to sit on Mother's bed in the living room, close together and talk, or rather yell, as the noise was so great. There the four of us were when CRASH! Glass crashed all over us, and something else banged down on us so we managed to light some matches to find that the window across the room had been crashed in by a big roof tile which had blown off the next building that was 500 feet away! Here was the bed covered with glass from the window that was clear across the room, and there lay three big broken jagged pieces of tile which had hit the bed hard enough to cut the sheets and not one of us was hurt, only Betts had a tiny scratch on her arm.

We were thankful! By this time it was 4:18 AM and water began to pour into the living room through the broken window in a solid sheet and under the porch doors from the porch. We had a long inside dressing closet, with no outside exposure at all, so Mother put a lot of pillows in there, and made Betts and me stay in there.

Luckily, she found another candle and brought it as this was a little victory to us, and believe it or not, we, too, sat there and played and sang till daylight, while the house swayed and shook, and everything outside let loose at once.

Meanwhile, Mother and Paul stripped the living room, which had become deep in water. The side next to the closet we were in was a little higher, so they could keep the water from running in on us. At 5 AM it was light enough to see out for the first time. We could only imagine how we each felt to look out and see palm branches, whole tops of pine trees, park benches, roofing, furniture, etc., flying through the air, while around our apartment was the ocean, big waves dashing against the house, and the water stretching for blocks further beyond us.

From 5:30 to 7:00 AM it was fierce, fierce, fierce with the water about 4 feet deep outside, and the waves much deeper and the water just rushing like mad. The wind was something terrible and the rain was coming down in sheets! Mother and Paul were as wet as if they'd been drowned for hours, and there was about 6 inches of water throughout the apartment except for the dressing closet which they had managed to keep dry for us, bless their hearts! We were afraid the foundation would give under the force of the water, as buildings were built right on the ground in Florida, but luckily it held.

About 8 AM the storm abated, wind died down, rain nearly stopped, and the tide receded leaving us surrounded by beautiful wet sand like a beach. A swirl of stranded, overturned autos, dozens of benches from across the street in the park, pines, palms, and what not, was a sight to behold!

Paul thought we ought to get in a little food as he didn't know how long the storm would abate sufficiently for us all to dare seek other quarters, so he started down to Piggly Wiggly about three blocks away. He had only been gone about 10 minutes when everything in the world let loose at once, and we all decided that, except for the darkness and high tide, the next storm was only a flicker beside this new one.

(EDITOR'S NOTE: Everyone thought that there were two storms very close together, but actually the eye of the storm passed over them, creating a quietness for a while, and then the other side of the hurricane came full force over them.)

In about 10 minutes, Paul got back in, staggered in, actually. He had been blown completely down and rolled over and over and skinned and cut on all sides, but was hanging onto a little bunch of supplies tied up tight in his soaking wet slicker. We found out the next day his arm was fractured.

All this time since early daylight all the other occupants of the house were screaming, and having hysterics and taking refuge in first one apartment, then another. Our apartment was a mess of wreckage by this time so we had to follow suit; we, all of us from our apartment, 22 all together, crowded in one apartment, and in a few minutes, CRASH! and then POW! the glass flew everywhere and cut some people.

We all would make a dash for another room and huddled together till we had to leave there. Everyone but Mr. Booth, who had charge of the apartments, and the four of us acted like darn fools. We soon discovered that the wind was raising the roof by getting into the blown-in apartments, and the rear wall had fallen out about 4 feet.

Pretty soon a big hunk of wall fell down onto and through the roof of the attached garage crushing a car completely, so the men decided it was time to move the women and children. There was a $91,000 brick house, boom price!, built and standing the storm so one of the men got over and burst in the back door as there seemed to be no one home, and so one by one we all managed to take refuge over in that strong big house.

The men took the women and children over one at a time, but Mother absolutely refused to be separated from us, or let us be separated from each other, so the three of us actually blew over together under Paul's guidance. How we did it we don't know. It seemed an impossible task to move the few steps from our house to the other house.

The wind was so great. It took three men to pull each person outside the door. The brick house had about 8 inches of water all over the lower floor and the upper floor was dripping like a rainstorm from the roof so there we were. Sitting around like frogs in a pond.

The women were still hysterical but Mother, Betts and I were getting a big kick out of it, having the grandest fun! We three waded into the living room and found a piano and piles of music and played for two hours, each one fighting for her turn at the keyboard!

Dozens of times we felt we could see the end, but as long as we could hold together, we weren't frightened. Mother was such a wonderful brick. I'll never forget it. She went around, cheering people up and making things so much easier for them.

Later in the day, the storm stopped, and we went back over to the apartment to pack what clothes we could save in bundles to carry on our backs and at about 3 PM we splashed down Meridian Avenue through high waters and wind to the Waverly Hotel on Fifth Street. The Stearns had the management of it and Mother knew they'd give us at least a mattress in the hall because they were good friends of ours and had two lovely daughters, Maxine and Libby, and we all were company for each other.

They were in pretty bad shape themselves, but all cheery, and made us very comfortable in a room almost dry and whole. We slept in a bed in bathing suits the first night, and then, as the rooms dried out and windows were put in, we got a room to ourselves.

For an entire week, Mother cooked for us in this one room, over alcohol in an empty condensed milk can, because she was afraid of typhoid if we ate out at the few restaurants that began opening. Lots of food began coming in and we could get drinking water, but it had to be boiled before we could drink it. We washed dishes in the wash basin in a spoonful of this precious water.

We were lucky to get in with the Stearns, because their car was practically totally injured in their garage, and it was quite a necessity to go back and forth to get the ice and water and food, etc. We had to carry along a 5 gallon water bottle for the water and stand in a long line to get it at the ice plant.

We had to have permits to get everything and could not buy more than two dollars worth at a time and Miami Beach was just put under Martial Law. We couldn't get over to Miami because the causeway was wrecked, and we had to be off the street by 7 PM. But people were brave and cheerful about it, so that the gigantic task of restoration and rebuilding was taken up immediately and was truly wonderful.

In a month, almost all traces of the storm had disappeared, but of course, things still looked awfully bare and scarred. It will take years and years to replace the palm trees and pines and shrubbery that blew away.

This hurricane was said to be one of the worst known in history . I'm glad I experienced it, but I shouldn't like to go through it again. At least it gave me pep and vitality enough to not think of my long hours of suffering with my infected ears, so it did one good deed if no other. (End of Hurricane.)

EDITOR'S NOTE: Hurricane of 1926 was also called a tropical cyclone and the winds reached 150 miles an hour. There were 600 fatalities and the damage was $105 million in the Miami area and that was back in 1926. In today's dollars, that would be $10.5 billion. 372 people died and 6,000 people were injured in the Miami area.

ADDITIONAL NOTE: May I say, as the editor (and very proud daughter,) I was extremely impressed with the writing ability of my mother, at age 16!

Great Miami Hurricane of 1926        Visit

Hurricane devastation.

Main road in Miami Beach.

Headlines in the New York Times.

Hurricane damaged apartment building in Miami Beach.

EDITOR'S NOTE: Throughout this collection of diary entries by my sweet mother, I have taken the liberty to google photos and information of different places and people she mentions. I felt this would be more interesting to my family when they read her diary to have visuals along the way of not only the Wheeler Twins but other people and places that touched their lives. Now, let's begin their show business journey into Vaudeville...

DIARY ENTRIES (Vaudeville, here we come!)

November 17, 1927. Went to Century theater to see if we could get in Max Reinhardt's "Midsummer Nights Drream". We were accepted after a wonderful audition. I'm so happy Mother is going to let us stop school.

EDITOR'S NOTE: The twins were 17 years old and I am guessing they just completed two months of their junior year of high school when their mother allowed them to quit school to be full-time professional dancers.

We went in at 10:30 this morning and we are going to be trees. We came too late to get really good dancing parts. But we really don't care; it's all such fun! Everybody is so precious and nice to us.

We rehearsed all day and all night until 2 AM. Dead tired. Only get $2 a performance, but it means a little Christmas money. We are loving this.

Dress rehearsal tonight. We got home at 2:30 AM. Opening night is tomorrow. All the seats are totally sold out and a very distinguished audience is expected. Surely hope they like this show!

Our opening night! Wonderful success! The audience cheered, and we had two curtain calls. The lights are not so good, but the costumes are very cute, like pajamas with feet. We have a hat with branches on it, and really look like trees!

Matinee today, big crowds. House packed solid tonight , wonderful write-ups in all the papers about it. We got paid tonight for five performances, $10. I hid it in my dressing room table.

In one of the numbers, Betty and I are torch boys. We sing, shout, dance, etc. Standing room only tonight, really really crowded.

Rehearsed this a.m. and then had a matinee this p.m. and another performance tonight. Midnight rehearsals from 12 midnight to 6 AM. I am dead tired, and oh so stiff.

Rehearsals from 11 AM to 3:30 PM today. In addition to our other numbers, we are in the first scene of act one, so that is really nice. Reinhart says we dance too much like girls. What in the world does he expect? Haven't seen our costumes for the new number yet.

Rehearsed from 10:30 AM till 6:30 PM tonight. The house was packed, wonderful success! Audience cheered and shouted for

Betty and me.

Slept till 1:30 PM today. Mother bought seven newspapers and we clipped the articles about the show. Very good. Washed my hair and feel like a new person.

Matinee today and a really packed house tonight. Diane wet her pants in the middle of her dance tonight. We laughed till we were weak and teased her about it.

Didn't go to rehearsal this morning. Just too tired. At the luncheon today Hines poured water in my basin and his partner threw some of it in my face, just for fun. But it made me furious.

I got mad at him for trying to make a fool of me at the banquet table. It wasn't necessary to do that. When he was not looking, I dropped an ice cold nickel down his back, and he really hollered, so our little fight is all over and peace is restored once more.

Rehearsed all day long and had dress rehearsal from 9 PM till 2 AM. Opening tomorrow night. We are to do a wild and woolly deaf dance in the last scene. That makes it all a lot crazier for us.

Opening was wonderful! Audience went hysterical and jumped out of their seats. 10 times better than our last show. Our dance was so cute and because Rinehart didn't think it was wild enough, but it may be put back in the show because the audience really seemed to love it.

The matinee was wonderful this afternoon. Very crowded house and the actors gave their best. Bought a "Vanity Fair" which had some great pictures of the show in it. This ends 1927.

July 31, 1928. Today is the day we started rehearsals with "Hold Everything" a huge well known famous production. We started learning the lyrics today and tomorrow we will start with all our dance numbers.

This is going to be fantastic and we are really in it to stay. This huge production has 12 tap dancers, 12 high kickers, 12 acrobatics, and 12 boys. We are two of the high kickers.

Luggage tag for performers in "Hold Everything"

Rehearsed from 11 AM to 5:30 PM today. Went to costumers to be fitted for opening number. Costumes are adorable. Night rehearsals begin tomorrow. Wow!

Went to equity early this morning before rehearsal and signed the book and all the necessary papers. The head manager Mac is really sweet. We get off from 5:00 to 8:00 so we'll come home for supper before the next rehearsal begins.

These day and night rehearsals are killing us. I think this show is going to be really good. We open in Newark for a week then to Philadelphia for two weeks and on and on from there hopefully.

Forgot to mention that I had my photos taken for the show. Saw my proofs. I'm really happy with them.

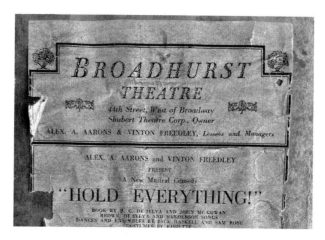

Put the first act together tonight with the "book" and it's really great. The show's gonna be a WOW! We all have such amazing costumes. However, I am dead tired!

Nothing new, except we're going straight through the show, the entire show, every day and night. We are rehearsing up until midnight every night and are beyond dead tired.

We open a week from today in Newark, New Jersey, and will have to stay in a hotel. Cost a lot, but it can't be helped.

Everything going great. We rehearsed this morning with all the scenery in place and with the live orchestra.

We started in with Festoff today. We take tap from him on Monday, Tuesday, Thursday, and Friday and ballet from his mother every single day at 3 o'clock. He is a wonderful dancer and has cute routines, but they are darn hard!

Billy sent me the sweetest letter this morning and he called me up and then met me after the show. So much attention is rather flabbergasting!

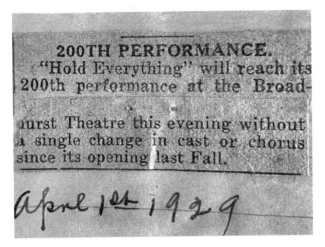

**200TH PERFORMANCE.**
"Hold Everything" will reach its 200th performance at the Broad-
urst Theatre this evening without a single change in cast or chorus since its opening last Fall.

*April 1st 1929*

Betty and I went to a call this afternoon for Schubert's "Sunny Days" but it was a show that went on the road and only paid $40 a week, so we did not even consider it. Betty's knee has been bothering her for the last two days, so she went to the doctor and he said the kneecap is broken. The bone is not broken, but a big gristle is torn that must knit the same as the bone. Her knee is now in a splint and she won't be able to get back to her dancing for at least a week. I hate to go to my lessons alone. I miss her so.

Joy and more joy! We went to Earl Carrol's call and all three of us wore the cute little practice dresses that Dot's mother made for us, and we all three were picked! Mr. Carrol liked us very much and spoke to us personally!

Mother started cute chiffon practice dresses for us for an interpretive dancing audition tomorrow. They might make a better impression with Mr. Carrol than the kind with stiff fluffy ruffles on them. We drove to Shepherds Bay this evening for the most grand fish dinner. It was pouring rain, but we didn't mind.

Wonderful shows today and tonight! Boston really likes us! Our names are up in lights, and it is so wonderful to look up and see! Three shows daily, and the last one is always at 1 AM. I am certainly exhausted!

Here we are, only 17 years old, and Mother allowed us to quit school to pursue our passion of dance! We went to school today and turned in all of our books. It is a big relief because our days and nights will be so full of costume fittings, rehearsals, and performances. We are working so hard, but it is entirely worth it, and we are professional and making money! We can hardly believe it! I believe our lives are going to be very exciting, and I hope we have the opportunity to travel too.

EDITOR'S NOTE: Youngest team in Vaudeville, Elinor and Elizabeth, with stage make up, at age 17.

A very well known artist picked us to pose for him, just head and shoulders, for an upcoming huge exhibit. He is very well known, has painted the Vanderbilts and such. The experience will be fine for us and we get $3.50 for half a day. I wish we could see the finished product!

After the last show tonight, Ray Nichols, who I met a couple nights ago, met me and we went to Leonard's to dance. He is the sweetest kid. I really like him so much.

EDITOR'S NOTE: This was the beginning of my mom and dad falling in love and this was June 24, 1931 and they married on January 20, 1937. 🖤

We opened tonight at the Stanley Theater in Jersey City. Ed Smith and Ray Nichols saw the last show and took us out afterwards. We went to a party at some friends of Ray's... Grand time! Ray is precious. He lives here in Jersey City.

Ed and Ray took us out after the last show again tonight. We went dancing some place over in Jersey. Very nice time. Going to see Ray all I can this week. He is so sweet!

The audience here has really been great. Dick Powell, the MC, is the nicest thing. Betty and I went out tonight with Dick, Paul, and a couple of his friends. Dick and I had to act as judges of a personality contest; we really had a fun time!

Dick Powell . Actor, musician, producer/director.

What a grand time we had again tonight. Dick Powell, Paul and his friend took us dancing. We went for a special ride in a speedboat too; it was such fun. Dick is so sweet. We are really having a great time here in Pittsburgh. I really hated to tell Dick goodbye. He certainly was sweet to us. Hope we get to work with him again sometime.

"Hold Everything"          Broadway

Betty is not feeling well . Her back gives her so much trouble! I have to go to equity all alone today. I miss it when she is not with me. I started on a new practice step today with my teacher. It's going to be real spiffy, you bet!

Betty is having more severe problems with her back and she went to the hospital tonight. She is going to be operated on tomorrow morning. We all went down with her. She certainly is game. I hated to leave her there alone. Mother and I broke down and balled when we got home.

Betty was operated on today. It was very successful. I was at the hospital with her all day … eight of us were there. Betts had a miserable day. She is in so much pain; in addition to her back, she had her appendix out and they found out she had a cyst on her ovary, and that was removed! I can only imagine how much she must have been suffering! I am all in myself tonight. I absolutely feel like a limp rag.

(Ten days later) Betts had all her stitches removed today. She has an 8 inch incision. She had a lot of visitors today, over eight people and the nurse would not let them see her. She is too tired and worn out and she has to lie on her back for five more days. Fifteen days in one position isn't too good. I am just about living at that hospital. I am there every day until 9 PM. This was the last day for Betty's special nurse. It broke her heart to give her up, but she must start helping herself a bit now.

It has been over two weeks now since Betty was operated on and she walked this afternoon for the first time. She walked down the hall and back. It took her over half an hour to make it. She was surely glad to get back in bed again.

Today is April 21, 1931 and we are 21 years old today. We expected Betts to be home from the hospital by today and we were going to have a big party, but she fooled us. However, we had a very lovely birthday in her hospital room. Hopefully, Betty will be home within one more week.

We brought Betts home from the hospital today after three weeks. The trip tired her quite a bit but she rested all day. She'll have to take it easy for a few weeks until she gets her strength back. Luckily. she has only lost 3 pounds.

It makes me so unhappy that Betts has so much back trouble. She just doesn't deserve it at all, and she has so much spunk! I do hope she recovers totally, and there's no more back trouble in her future.

Elizabeth (Betty)

We had rehearsal with the orchestra again today and it is so much better now. Had dress rehearsal tonight and Mr. Freedley said we will have to work all night in order to open on Monday. No more sleep for us! Bert Lahr and Olivette are the best in the show. They are the comedians. This show here in New York City has been great but this is our last day. Tomorrow we have to be at the Shubert Theater in Newark."

Bert Lahr (1895 – 1967)

EDITOR'S NOTE: Bert Lahr was in 17 Hollywood movies, his most favorite was portraying the cowardly lion in the "Wizard of Oz ". While filming a Hollywood movie in 1967, in the cold rain late at night, he contracted pneumonia and died at only 72 years of age.

The twins mother, Wilna.

Mother and Daddy came today and we gave Mother a lovely pin for her birthday which was last Sunday. We paid $16.50 for it. She is so worth it! She is just so fun and keen on everything we accomplish! Hated to see them go because I get so homesick.

We are rehearsing a new song. "Step This Way"; it is really great. Last night I fell jumping down the stairs, but I got up and kept on going. The house was really packed tonight.

Gave an audition today and the job is ours! The Concourse Plaza, a big hotel is putting on an extravagant new show. Saw Ray tonight and we went to NBC broadcasting studio. Went downtown this afternoon to get some fabric and costume stuff for Mother. She has to finish six costumes in two weeks, bet she can't do it! Tramped all over New York trying to get some music for our new dance. Finally had to order it. Saw Ray tonight and we went over to New Jersey to a place to eat and dance. He is so sweet!

Did a lot of last-minute shopping for tomorrow's opening night. Got a high silk hat and a cane, also a beautiful new suit. Had the grand opening tonight and it was a howling success. We went over like a million dollars each show. We're headlining at every theater now.

WHEELER TWINS & BOUCHE VILLA VENICE
Miami Beach
1 March 1932

Really good shows tonight. Saw Ray between shows and we took a long drive. I wore my new suit; it looks stunning. It's a reddish orange, trimmed in raccoon.

Rain, rain, rain all day and night. Saw Ray between shows tonight. Feels rather funny not seeing Billy anymore, but I have no desire to.

Billy called me up tonight and insisted on seeing me but I wouldn't let him. There's not a thing he can do or say that will bring him back in my good graces. He has had too many chances.

Walter Winchell (1889 - 1972)

EDITOR'S NOTE: He left school at age 13, and became a vaudeville performer and later a syndicated American newspaper gossip columnist, and radio news commentator. Very famous!

Saw Ray between shows . Had a big banquet tonight in honor of Walter Winchell, the place was really jammed. Walter Winchell is good looking.

Great shows tonight. Ray came between shows with Ed and his girl Lee and we all went to the Inn together. Had so much fun. Got slightly tipsy on beer. Had a good time doing the last show though!

Al Jolson (1886 - 1957)

EDITIOR''S NOTE: American singer and black face comedian, and was in the first talking picture, "The Jazz Singer".

Beatrice Lily and Al Jolson were at the show tonight. We enjoyed visiting with both of them between shows. They said they really enjoyed our dancing so much. We're doing great business. Papers all say it is the best musical show in New York.

EDITOR'S NOTE: Black lace costumes trimmed in fur designed and made by their mother, Wilna Wheeler, (my Nana), who was also the wardrobe head for Paramount Studios and sewed magnificent costumes for the silent movie stars, and then for the talkies.

Mother Wilna, Wardrobe head for Paramount Studios

Started our eccentric high kick routine with Buddy Bradley today at the theater. He's one of the specialty dancers and has given us some wonderful grand stuff.

A terrible thing happened tonight. Mother slipped on a rug and broke her right ankle. The big outside ankle bone broken clear through and a ligament is torn clear away and the inside flesh is all torn. So awful! Poor darling Mother! She had her ankle set and has to keep it in a plaster cast for at least six weeks. It pains her so and she can't manage to get around at all on crutches. She is so discouraged. I wish I had it instead.

All great shows today, but Burt Lahr's wife is expecting a baby any day and he is so worried and nervous that he can't do anything right!

Ray and Elinor

Saw my Ray between shows tonight. How I love him! Wish we could get married. (EDITOR'S NOTE: They married six years later in 1937)

Billy called me today and he is still pleading with me to see him but I'll be darned if I will. I can hold my own against him anytime!

What a wonderful time I had today. Ed and Lee and Ray and I went to the Army/Notre Dame game, Army won 12 to 0. Then dinner and a big formal dance. Ray is so precious.

My sweet Ray came by tonight. Love him so. He sure makes every effort to see me as much as he can, even though he works very hard on Wall Street. He is also very dedicated to his mother, as his father died of pneumonia when he was only seven years old. He became the man of the house, and his mother depends on him so much and they are very dedicated to each other. She is a wonderful lady. They are very Catholic and never miss Mass.

Had such a nice time. Met Ray down on Wall Street, where he works and we had lunch together. Then he showed me all around. Had to leave him to make a 2 o'clock show. Shucks!

PHIL LEARNS TO DANCE!

Phil Harris, motion picture star and bandmaster at the College Inn, learns about dancing from the beautiful Wheeler twins, Betty and Eleanor—the accomplished dancing duo now appearing in the Harris show at the Hotel Sherman's bright spot. Phil's hoping that this dancing lesson won't be electrically transcribed to the nation.

Chicago American
Oct. 25, 1933.

Phil Harris, Bandleader (1904 - 1995)

We totally love working with Phil Harris in his big show. He is beyond charming and so complimentary to us!

Got a little more Christmas shopping done today. Bought Ray some lovely hankies with open work and monograms on them. The old sweet thing.

Ray Francis Nichols, future husband!

Buddy Bradley, choreographer.

EDITOR'S NOTE: Buddy Bradley was an African-American dancer and choreographer from the early 30's through the 50's. His students included Fred Astaire and Ruby Keeler, as well as the Wheeler twins! When it came to tap dancing, he liked his students to move across the stage rather than hoof in the spot. He did the choreography for "Anything Goes", a Broadway show in which the Wheeler twins performed. He died at the age of 58 while undergoing brain surgery.

Started working again with Buddy Bradley. He is an amazing teacher, and we can understand why he is so expensive. We work very hard for him. Every hour counts! He says we do our dance just like one person now. It's about time!

Went down to see about the Florida job, but they're undecided yet. I guess we're not going. My precious Ray came to see me tonight. Didn't go out, but had lots of fun. Gee, I love him.

We signed the contract today for the Villa Venice in Miami Beach. We leave Monday, hooray! I had lunch with Ray today. I sure will hate to leave him on Monday!

On our way to Miami Beach now. Sailing on the "Savannah City". This is one awful trip. The boat is so tiny and there's nothing to do on board. We get to Savannah Thursday morning and then change to a train and get into Miami Thursday night. Ran into a rain storm and very rough seas.

Still going. Running into warm weather now. Play deck games all afternoon. This is a lousy trip. Get into Savannah at 5 AM tomorrow morning. I miss Ray so much. Wish he were with me. I won't see him for so long.

Changed to a train at Savannah and got in Miami at 7 PM. So glad to be here. Living at 1017 Jefferson Ave. on the beach. Awfully tired tonight.

EDITORS NOTE: All throughout my mother's 12 diaries, she often gives exact addresses of the "cute apartments" that they move into often during their extensive travels in show business. I googled at least five of these addresses, but now they are towering 20 story condominiums, and the "cute apartments "are no longer there..... of course...... 90 years later!

And today is Christmas day and we're all alone for the first time. Christmas is funny in Florida. So hot. Ray gave me a beautiful wrist watch. I felt so awful about it. It was much too much!

We started rehearsals tonight. The club is really nice. Bouche' fired the orchestra, but I guess they'll all be friends by tomorrow again. He has a temper from time to time. It was a nice sunny day today but very windy. I sent out a lot of New Year's cards.

Albert "Papa" Bouche' (1881-1964)

EDITOR'S COMMENT: Bouche' came from Italy to New York City and worked as a cook in his younger years and later opened his first magnificent restaurant and nightclub and several years later he came to Miami Beach and opened his second and equally spectacular Villa Venice.

EDITOR'S COMMENT: Fact: Bouche' came to New York from Italy and became a cook. Fiction: his obituary stated he "came to the United States in 1920, working as an interpreter in five languages. ". Not true! 😂😂

Bob Hope 1903 - 2003 (100 years old!)

EDITOR'S NOTE: After I raised the money for the King Center for the Performing Arts in Melbourne, FL, we hired Bob Hope to perform there. I visited with him for at least 30 minutes in the stars private lounge (green room) before the show and even though he was getting quite forgetful in his 80's, he was absolutely charming. His wife, Deloris, was also lovely, and was very helpful to him in his forgetfulness.

Another fun EDITOR'S COMMENT: In 1927, Bob Hope went to Albert Bouche' at Villa Venice and auditioned for the job of emcee-comic. Bouche' said "Sorry, you won't do, but have a steak on me. "

One last EDITOR'S COMMENT about Villa Venice is... Later years, after the Wheeler twins performed there, the Rat Pack (Sammy Davis, Jr., Dean Martin, Frank Sinatra, and Joey Bishop ) appeared there at the same venue

December 31, 1931. We opened tonight and everything was a huge success! Betts and I were the talk of the entire place. Everyone said we were a sensation. Feel so sad tonight. 😢 I wish I could be home with Ray. Happy New Year.

Another year ended and once again, I am far from home. But I am happy here in Miami as I've wanted to come back here for five years and this year has given me Ray Nichols, and through him a great deal of happiness. I thought I loved Billy Blaine, but I was wrong. My love for Ray is real; I am sure. All I know is that I adore him. This is the end of my diary and the end of 1931. Tomorrow I start a new one.

The Wheeler, Twins, 22 years old, 1932.

1932

Here I am starting a new year and a new diary, and in Miami Beach at that. It is so glorious here! We opened up Bouche's Villa Venice last night, and everything was a huge success. Betty and I were the talk of the place. I haven't heard from Ray in three days and I am getting worried.

Had the most wonderful letters from Ray today! It cheered me up a lot. I'm so homesick and lonesome for him.

I took my first aeroplane ride today. The new 21 passenger Curtis Condor was making its maiden flight and we were invited to go up as a publicity stunt. It was so thrilling.

EDITOR'S NOTE: Curtis Condor aeroplane. 1930's. US Army bi-plane bomber, also used for transport.

Two wonderful letters from Ray today. It surely makes me feel grand when I hear from him. Had such a long hard rehearsal tonight. Went through both shows a couple times. Didn't get home until 4:30 AM.

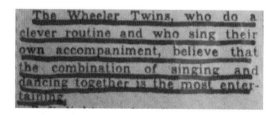

The Wheeler Twins, who do a clever routine and who sing their own accompaniment, believe that the combination of singing and dancing together is the most entertaining.

Gave both shows tonight and Betts and I stopped the show on all our numbers. It was grand. We do our kick number in the first show, and our waltz and pajama dance in the second show; we were the hit of the show all right. What a glorious feeling! Now another week of rehearsals and then we have our grand opening of this huge show in Miami Beach. It will be good to start drawing a salary.

EDITOR'S NOTE: For the Villa Venice venue, the twins (and all performers) were paid nothing for all the rehearsals, they were just paid per performance of the actual ticketed shows.

EDITOR'S NOTE: Anton Cermak, the mayor of Chicago. He was injured by an assassin's bullet intended for President-elect Franklin Delano Roosevelt. He died 19 days after the shooting of a perforated colon. (see diary entry below.)

Oh, what a ridiculous day this has been. Dreary and gray to begin with, and we all, including the orchestra, had to tramp down to the station to meet the mayor of Chicago, Anton Cermak, who is a good friend of Bouche'. It was so silly. I felt stupid. Then we were called for rehearsal tonight and didn't do a darn thing. The mayor and his party came in drunk, really drunk, so Bouche' let us all go home. Sweet of him.

Took a terrible fall in the second show. Fell on my head and knocked myself unconscious. Everybody scared to death, including the audience, but I went on for the next performance, and stopped the show with thunderous applause! I really made the effort to do the next performance, and the audience made it all worthwhile, and it kind of brought me to tears with their gratitude.

Funny story, two big parties in stunning evening clothes came to the club tonight, It was rehearsal, but they did not know. So Bouche' let them stay and watch the actual dress rehearsal. They evidently thought the place was open and enjoyed it completely, and were ever so surprised when Bouche' did not charge them any money! (Did they even wonder why there was no one else in the audience?)

What a party! This is Mr. Bouche's birthday, and he threw a tremendous party at the club, over 200 invited guests. We had to give both shows, but joined the party later. We girls got corsages from Bouche', and there were tons of champagne and all kinds of liquors and a marvelous supper. He certainly did it up in grand style and we didn't get home till 6 AM.

Took Betty to the doctor today. Her back has slipped out of place again, and she can hardly work. She had an electric treatment, and now her back is all blistered. Has to go back tomorrow for another treatment, poor kid.

Poor Betty had lots of back problems

Rain, rain all day long and of course Bouche' would call a 4 o'clock rehearsal. Betty went to the doctor again and he strapped her back good. I think the bone slipped back in place but it still hurts like the dickens. She has to go again tomorrow.

Betty's back slipped out again. I wish she could lay off for a while. It hurts her so very badly. It makes me feel awful for her.

Betty's back got much worse today. She was all bent over double and in such agony. We got her to the doctor and he set her spine again and strapped her up good. She must lay off several days at least. I went on alone tonight. I felt so lonesome. I was nervous too. I never worked alone before. Mr. Bouche' made an announcement that one of the Wheeler Twins was ill, so the audience understood.

Dancing alone... No fun for me.

Mother took Betts to the doctor again. She won't be able to work till week after next. So I must hold the fort all alone. I did a fine trick tonight. During the last show, I got a terrible seize of cramps and started throwing up all over the place. I also missed the finale and I really tried, but could not make it work. Bouche' didn't know what the dickens was wrong. But there were very sympathetic people backstage.

Packed audience tonight, such nice people. Didn't eat till after the third show so it was 5:30 AM by the time I got to bed. I'm sick of this job already. The hours are too darn hard. No letter from my Ray today, darn it. I'm so homesick. Betty feels quite a bit better today. She's anxious to be back to work, but she must wait about a week.

Mother brought Betts over for the first show tonight. They didn't tell me they were coming. They didn't want me to be nervous. I saw them during the finale, and went out and joined them between shows. Betts was quite thrilled seeing me work alone. Her back is improving a lot. She may be able to come back to work next week.

Betty's back got so much worse today. She had an awful time. Mother and I are worried to death. Don't think she'll be able to dance anymore, at least not for several weeks anyway. Bouche' said I could go on alone and he would pay me half salary. That will at least help us down here while we are in Miami Beach so that she can rest and get well. Got two dozen lovely tea roses today. Had very very good shows tonight and a great audience.

Bouche' found out that Sally Rand was out last night after the show and didn't get home till 7 AM. So there was a big battle today and he fired her. Ahi, who was out with her, said she'd leave if Sally was fired. And one thing led to another, so Papa Boo changed his mind and took Sally back. He kills me. Pretty good shows tonight.

EDITOR'S NOTE: Sally Rand (1904 to 1979) was a dancer known for her ostrich feather fan dance. Studied ballet and drama. Cecil B DeMille gave her the stage name inspired by the Rand McNally atlas.

EDITOR'S NOTE: Although Sally Rand never performed nude, she often wore long tight flesh colored underwear that gave that appearance. She died at age 73.

Betty did everything tonight in the shows. The kick number tired her out quite a lot, but it even wears me down. Marvelous crowds. Business is getting better and better and the crowds are huge. Our contract reads 12 weeks. We expect to stay on down here a couple of weeks after we close so we can get a good rest and tan. The time is going much faster than I expected.

Did a benefit tonight for the unemployed. We do not get paid for it, but it is for a good cause. We were headlined with Helen Morgan. Had two swims today and what with four shows tonight, I'm dead tired. Too sweet letters from Nickie boy.
Our photos were in the paper again today. They are in nearly every day. We are the only ones who are getting a lot of publicity.

EDITOR'S COMMENT: Helen Morgan did not complete her elementary school education, but became an actress on stage and films. She mostly sang songs of heartbreak and hard living. Helen was best known as Julie in the Broadway musical Showboat in 1927. An alcoholic, she died of cirrhosis of the liver at age 41.

Betty and Elinor Wheeler are the dancing stars of Pierre Nuytien's revue, presented nightly in the Silver Forest of the Drake Hotel. (Seymour photo.)

Another scorching day today in Miami even though it is only February. A lot of the girls went to the solarium to get some sunburn and the poor kids came in to work looking like beef steak! Bouche' gave them hell and said the next person caught on the beach or in swimming would be fined $10. They put whiting on though, and looked all right for the show.

Betts and I had to dance at the famous Surf Club tonight between shows. A beautiful place, but that's the last benefit we do. Bouche' gets paid for it and we don't get a thing out of it. It's nice of us to do it but with three shows a day, it is absolutely too much for us.

Betty is getting the grippe, I think. Poor darling. As soon as she gets over one thing, something else pops up. She has a terrible cold now and it's settling all over her. The insurance company paid her $80 today for what she's already paid to the doctors, and they'll pay the doctors the rest. Thank goodness for that. She felt so badly tonight she couldn't go on for the last show. Had quite a fever and the first two shows just about knocked her out.

Just another empty day, without any mail or anything, but then again, it is Sunday. I'm beginning to take a big shine to Freddie Daw, one of the musicians. A little harmless flirtation won't hurt, and it will keep me from going jittery. He's so sweet and he likes me a lot too. I hope we can have a couple of dates together without disobeying any rules.

Mother, Betts and I went into town today and had a gay time. Bought some material, some cute blue stuff and I'm going to start a dress. Got the pattern I wanted. It will be something to do between shows. I'm so sick of playing bridge.

Ready to go for a relaxing swim.

Went swimming with Freddie today. We had to sneak way down the beach where no one from the Villa would see us. The girls and the musicians aren't even supposed to talk to each other. We had a grand time and I surely like him. He's only 23 and he is married and has a precious baby. But it's just a nice little friendship between us.

Mr. Boo (Bouche') called us all over to the club today and gave us a lecture. He doesn't want any of the girls to even talk to the musicians. He certainly is bitter against them for some reason or other. He said Freddie Daw was the only gentleman in the band. I'm glad he likes Freddie because I think he's a peach.

Had pretty good shows tonight, but there was quite a storm. The lights kept going out, and we could only do half of our numbers in the dark. It was fun!

A cold raw day today. I slept till 4 PM and caught up on my rest. I was so tired and I found out I have lost 6 pounds. Down to 112 again, and I'm disgusted with myself. Was 118 pounds and I wanted to get to 120, but of course I had to lose. After we close, I'll gain again I guess.

I am going to meet Freddie Daw tomorrow and go to a movie or a drive with him. He certainly is a peach! Had three sweet letters from Ray. Hadn't heard from him for two days and guess I won't get one tomorrow. I wish the letters wouldn't double up that way.

Met Freddie today, and we took a long drive, 53 miles. Talked so much we didn't realize how far we were going. Got back just in time to go to the club for supper. Had lots of fun. But I didn't hear from my sweet Ray today.

Pretty good shows tonight. The cool weather seems to bring people in. I don't feel too grand lately. Haven't been eating much and I don't feel so well. I can hardly dance.

Was I mad today! We got up at 8:30 this morning to go to a sale on Lincoln Road, and it didn't amount to a thing. It was so bitterly cold, we could hardly get there. Had to walk as the car wouldn't start. The things they had weren't worth a nickel. So home we came and slept all day. Can't understand what's wrong with our car. Every night we have to be pushed to get it going. They can't find the trouble at the garage.

What a funny night! The place was jammed! Had the Yachtsman Regatta supper there and what a crowd. The orchestra went on strike tonight until Boo paid them their money. We got paid that first week. He held out on the orchestra though.

Well, thank goodness our job at the Villa Venice has finally exhausted itself and we're all finished. I thought it would never end. Three shows every night are just a lot! And we do three dances in each show... Got all my junk carried home, never knew I had so much. Freddie gave me a drink, so we were feeling gay. Now for a grand rest, and a good time. So long, Villa Venice!

Interior of Villa Venice, Miami Beach, Florida

My first free night in a long, long time. Since before last Christmas actually. Didn't waste it either. Went out with Freddie and got caught in the pouring rain. Took a ride with him this afternoon. He is going back to Chicago day after tomorrow. Gee, I hate to think of it. I wonder if we'll ever meet again. I'm going to hope that we will. Packed a lot today. Going to move tomorrow.

Moved today to a nice apartment in Miami. Freddie and his family decided to leave tomorrow instead of today, so I had one more happy day with him. We were both busy packing, but it was fun running into him every few minutes. My heart is just numb tonight. He is just such a special friend to me and telling him goodbye was the hardest thing I ever did. We both cried like babies. Please let me see him soon again.

This day has been agony for me. I can't realize that Freddie is gone and I can't go meet him on the beach or take rides with him anymore. I cried all last night and today. The whole world seems empty now. I guess I'll get over it, of course, but I've never felt this way before. Thought I'd feel better if I went out tonight, so I took a ride with Billy Dozier and was bored to death. I started a letter to Freddie and cried so hard I could hardly finish it.

Feel a little better today although my heart still aches so badly. I rented a radio for the month and it is grand. We certainly missed having one. Only five dollars a month rental. Betty has a terrible sore all over her mouth. Has to stay in bed several days. Poor kid, it is always something with her.

Didn't do a thing today except drive Madame Queen, our Chevy, awhile. Getting used to it for the trip home. Betty's been doing most of the driving down here, so now I must get used to the antics of it.

1932 Chevy coupe that the Wheeler twins fondly named "Madame Queen ".

I had two letters from my sweet Ray today. I felt so low tonight. I have been so lonesome for Freddie all day. I'd give anything just to hear his voice. I've never missed anyone like this before.

EDITOR'S NOTE: These diary entries are blowing me away! Elinor, my mother, married Ray Nichols in 1937, AND.....my mother's twin sister, Betty, married Freddie Daw in 1945!!!!! Wow!

Today is my birthday, and I am 22 years old. And I would like to stay this way for the rest of my life! Daddy sent me stockings and four boxes of candy. Mother gave us beautiful bags and hankies, and we gave each other purses. Ray forgot my birthday, not even a card. Had a wire from Billy and a darling card from Freddie. I wrote him a long letter tonight.

Biltmore Country Club and Hotel, Coral Gables, Florida (1932)

I had the best time in my whole entire life tonight! The Biltmore Country Club and Hotel in Coral Gables had a big dance tonight and Dr. Gibbs invited us to join his party. Such nice people and we had such a glorious time. Dr. Gibbs had never seen us dance, so we did one number out there, "Tea for Two" and we were a sensation! Got to bed at 6 AM.

EDITOR'S NOTE: Twenty years later, (1950's) Betty worked for Dr. Gibbs, who was a chiropractor, as his receptionist! This was in Coral Gables, Florida.

Going to a dance at the Coral Gables Country Club Saturday night. Got a box of beautiful roses from Chris this morning. A new kind of tea rose that he named the "Elinor Rose".

EDITOR'S NOTE: Twenty-eight years later from the entry above, I married Bob Kirk (we were both 19 years old) and we had our wedding reception for over 200 people at the Coral Gables Country Club!

Coral Gables Country Club. 1932 and 1985

We are going to open in Boston Saturday for a week, but we must all work on a cut. Betts and I will make $150 instead of $200, but it will give us a little to pay off bills and get the car fixed. If we go to Florida, by the time we get back from Boston, Bouche' will be here, and we'll see what's what. Ray came over tonight. I got our trunk off this morning and we leave for Boston tomorrow.

In Boston now, our fourth time here. Don't open until tomorrow. Staying at the LaSalle Hotel where we always stay when we're here. We saw the show at the Memorial tonight. I try to get in touch with Lou Walters to see if we could double at a club while we are here, but we won't be able to see him until tomorrow.

Opened today and the act is going over great. Had supper tonight with Lou Walters at the Cascades. It was on the rooftop and a lovely club, part of the Bradford Hotel. We're going to double there starting Monday night. He's only paying us $90. It helps out because we're working on a cut this week and only getting $150 from him. There are two shows a night at the Cascades, 7:30 PM and 11 PM., So we can make it fine. Four a day....We can make it work at the theater and two shows more at the Cascades.

What a funny day! They have the blue law here in Boston, so although they have shows, no one can dance! Only three shows, but all we did was walk in and do a pose. Rather funny, putting on our shoes and costumes and makeup for that! The audience still seemed to like it very much. The law is the law. Went to bed early and got a good rest. Snowing hard... Phoned mother for our galoshes.

Oh dear, what a hard day! Our first day of doubling. Had a little trouble with our music at the club on the first show, but the last show was grand and we stopped the show with our kick number. Just do two numbers, and the pajama dance. We're in the finale too. Good orchestra and a good floor to work on and have a really nice people in the audience. Letters from Freddie and Ray today.

I felt dead tired all day. Could hardly work. The strain of doubling is beginning to be felt by now. I took a different set of costumes over to the club. The white pajamas made a big hit. Paul Ash was at the last show and invited us to sit at his table. Lou Walters was there, and Henry Drake and Bill Taylor came in later. Had a good time. Home at 3:00 AM. Letter from Ray and Daddy.

EDITOR'S NOTE: I meant to mention it before, but Lou Walters was BarbaraWalters father. Barbara was only three years old and was with her dad from time to time and my mother and Betty loved playing with her.

Closed at the Memorial today, but we don't close at the Cascades until tomorrow night. Our last day of the doubling, thank goodness! I don't mind saying I am all in. Had another letter from Ray, but didn't hear from Freddie. Thought surely I would.

Our contract's over and then we go to New York. Got into New York at 7:30 AM, dead tired. Didn't sleep a wink on the train last night. Slept all day, then went down to the Casino Theater and gave an audition for the new George White Varieties. Tom showed us the whole act and he liked it, and he's going to use us, but he's going to put our numbers in a certain spot in the show. It will be better that way. I am so tickled. It means we can't go to Florida this year this year but I don't care.

EDITOR'S NOTE; Tom Patricola, 1891 to 1950. American actor, comic and dancer. Starred in Vaudeville and motion pictures. He was the director of the George White Follies, starring the Wheeler twins.

September, 1932.

Well, today is over, and what a day!

Another day gone. We are now doing four shows today and it is a huge theater. Packed every show. Ray and I went to the Roosevelt Grill and Guy Lombardo and his Orchestra are playing there. It was so crowded and we danced and danced and loved it so much. Guy Lombardo has seen us dance and has given us many nice compliments!

Guy Lombardo

Did some more shopping today. Got some hats and some darling sport shoes for the boat. We sail at 4 PM on Saturday.

EDITOR'S NOTE: (September 1932) Beginning the journey to Paris, France, and then to London, England, to perform!

On our way at last. We were disappointed in the boat. It's not as new as we expected, but it certainly is huge. Our rooms aren't so hot either, but we didn't pay our fare, so what can we expect? Had a whole gang down to see us off. Ray gave me three dozen gorgeous tea roses, and I didn't discover them till after we sailed.

Got books and candy from the others. The sea is like a pond, hardly a ripple. Hope it's this way the whole trip. Our boat is called the SS Paris.

S S Paris

Our second day at sea. It passed very quickly. Couldn't change our rooms to first class, but got another room next to the one we have now so we have plenty of room between the two of us. We have the run of the whole ship, so it doesn't matter much where we sleep. The sea is still awfully calm. I expected it to be rougher.

I'm beginning to get tired of this trip now. I wish it were over. Three days on the ocean is enough for me. I don't think we'll get to land before Saturday. This is a slow boat, this S. S, Paris. Did a lot of letter writing today. Had the doctor look at my sore throat. It's still troubling me. I had an inhalation treatment and some medicine for it.

Gee, I'm bored. I'm even getting cross and rude. I didn't want to come on this trip in the first place, the sooner we get back home the better. I am homesick already, and I am only as far as the middle of the ocean. I'll be happy to get off this darn boat. It just seems so slow.

Another long day at sea. I finished a book and wrote some letters. I limbered up in the gym for a while. We have a big performance tomorrow night. Joined a cocktail party just before supper and had a very good time tonight. Went upstairs to dance.

Photo of S. S. Paris program

Didn't do much today. The performance tonight was really very good. They took the ship off its course for an hour, while the show was on, so it wouldn't dip so much. We did our pajama dance because it was the easiest one to do on a moving stage! We were afraid we would fall on the other dances. Tonight was the last big night. Tomorrow we get to Plymouth, England.

It was certainly good to see land today. We reached Plymouth, England, about 3 o'clock and we get to our next destination about 2 AM tomorrow morning. Our train to Paris leaves at 7 o'clock so we can sleep till six. It's been a lovely trip but I'll be glad to get on land again. Had a nice write-up in the ship's paper about our dance last night. Everything is quite dead today, the last day.

Well, well, well! Our first day in Paris is over. We got in at 2 AM and stayed on the boat till 7;30 then we took the train. Staying at the Moderne Hotel and it is so nice. None of us are a bit disappointed in Paris. It is so quaint and lovely. Mother is terribly excited. We open at the Alhambra next Friday, so we have a good long rest. We visited the theater tonight and it's really a lovely theater .

Alhambra Theatre 1866 to 1967

EDITOR'S NOTE: 600 seat music hall. Duke Ellington, and many famous performers were featured here.

Our first Sunday in Paris. We spent a very lazy day as there was nothing open today. Stayed in the hotel until six, then we went out to eat. Spent the day unpacking and writing letters. We have very nice connecting rooms here and a bath, 90 francs a day equals $3.60.

EDITOR'S NOTE: At this lovely hotel in Paris, they had two separate bedrooms and a connecting bathroom for a total of US

$3.60 a day! Holy moly, I would love to price those two rooms with connecting bath at a Paris Hotel today at 2023 prices!

Had such a glorious time tonight. We went with the William Morris agent to the Casino de Paris, and saw the review entitled "Sex Appeal of 1932." Then we went to the Mont Marte Club, one of the smartest clubs in Paris. Irving Berlin was there and Maurice Chevalier and several princes were there as well. There was an American orchestra playing.

EDITOR'S NOTE: Casino de Paris. Opened in 1890 and is a 2,057 seat performance venue, not a gambling house, even though the name "casino".

EDITOR'S NOTE; Irving, Berlin, famous composer, who wrote "Blue Skies ", White Christmas", and many more.

EDITOR'S NOTE: Maurice Chevalier, an extremely popular French movie star, most famous for co-starring in the movie "Gigi" with Audrey Hepburn many years later.

Had another exciting day. We went downtown and spent the whole afternoon taking everything in. Spent most of our time viewing the shops . We saw a very nice gentleman (huge millionaire!) who we met when we were on the boat and he took us cocktailing and we toured the highlights of Paris. What a lovely man, and such a gentleman.. We are learning to speak a little French. Ended our day by going to the Follies Bergère , disappointed in it.

1930s poster of the Follies Bergère.

Mother's ticket from the Follies Bergère.

October 19, 1932. Spent a very quiet day, slept till very late. Mother sewed all day and Betts read. Didn't even leave the hotel until we went out for supper. Have a rehearsal tomorrow at 10 AM. I do so hope there will be a letter at the theater from Ray. I am so homesick for him.

Had a rehearsal this morning. Took two hours just to rehearse our act. The musicians are all French, and only the orchestra leader speaks English, so it took a long time. The 25 piece orchestra is truly fabulous.

At last we have opened. Had two shows, 3:00 and 9 o'clock. Our act is in the last half of the program. Had to cut everything out except for dancing. All the comedy and talk is out. These French people don't understand English! The audience is tough but our numbers go over well. Mother saw the show tonight, says it's a great bill. Have really nice dressing rooms. It's really very good to be working again and fun to be in France!

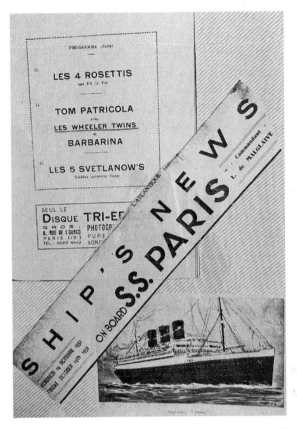

Had three shows today, two and five and 9 o'clock. The afternoon shows are a joke, only a tiny handful of people in the audience. But the 9 o'clock show is beyond packed. Our number went over beautifully tonight. We go over even better than we ever imagined. Tom informed us that we will be paid in English pounds instead of francs or American money so that cuts about 1/3 off our salary. Instead of $200 we will get $125, don't see how we can manage.

Three more shows today and I'm dead tired tonight. The supper show was the only bad show. It rained tonight so it kept a lot of people home. On the last show tonight, Betts got mixed up in the curtain somehow and couldn't get out for a bow with all of us. Barbara and I had to take it alone with Tom. What a mess. I have a terrible cold; the weather is so changeable here.

Mr. Pennypacker, a young American millionaire over here, and a friend of Jack Dempsey, came to see us in our show, and we had a grand time with them tonight. Henry Clement, and Dyck Levon, a couple more millionaires, whom we met on the boat, took us out tonight. we went to the Mont Marte Club. Had so much fun. Didn't get home till 5:30 AM. Going out with them again on Thursday.

Got paid last night. Tom wanted to cut our salary $60 but we wouldn't take it. He's getting paid in pounds and it's so much less than anything else. We have a contract with him for $200 a week, and he's got to give it to us. Had a good time after the show. We all went to the Lido, a beautiful night club with a swimming pool in it. Very unusual.

Three shows today. The extra one surely tires us out. I don't know what we'd ever do if we had to do five a day like we do in the states. Went out again tonight with Clem. Had more fun than I've had so far. Got home early. I'm really getting sick of Paris. I'll be glad to get out of here. It is a beautiful city with a lot of history, but we work so hard.

All three shows were great today, especially the last one. Had a packed house. Three boats get in from America tomorrow, hope there's some mail on them for me.

Had such a good show tonight. The English football team was out front and did they love our act! We just about stopped the show! Tomorrow is our last day at the Alhambra, thank goodness. It's been a long two weeks here especially since I'm not receiving any mail from the states.

Our last day at the Alhambra. Didn't have much of an audience. Tom tripped me in the finale, and I fell flat on my face. Things always happen on the last show somehow. We leave for London tomorrow. Maybe there will be some mail for us there.

November 1933. London, England.

In London now. Had a terrible trip. So slow. Left Paris at 10 this morning and got in at seven tonight. The trip across the channel was quite rough. Nearly everyone was sick. But we all managed to keep our dignity. Cold and pouring rain. I think I'm going to like London, it reminds me a lot of New York. Anything would be a relief after Paris. Staying at the Regent Paris hotel. A lovely place. Only seven minute walk from the Palladium where we will be dancing. Stopped at the theater but unfortunately, there was no mail for us.

Spent most of the day looking for a cheaper place to live, but they all seem to be the same and the Regent Palace is the closest to the theater so I guess we'll just stay there. Tried to see the show at the Palladium tonight, but all the seats were sold out. We went to a movie instead, a German picture entitled "M". The most wonderful thing I've ever seen. All about a child murderer.

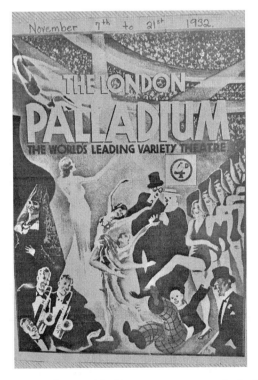

We open at the London Palladium tomorrow. It is known as the most wonderful and important vaudeville house in all the world so we're very nervous about it.

What a day! Opened at the Palladium and went over a big! Never had such applause in all of our lives! Tom, our manager, is tickled pink. Two weeks of this is going to be a pleasure. Our act is headlining over 14 other acts. We have two shows a night, 6:30 and 9:00 PM and a matinee on Wednesday and Thursday. We have the sweetest little dressing room, all done in rose and yellow. Got some lovely flowers today; it's going to be a great two weeks!

Oh, today is November 11, Armistice Day, and they certainly are patriotic over here in Europe. Betty hurt her back last night in the show, and she could hardly work tonight. Had to have a doctor between shows who said all of her back muscles were badly torn. I don't think she'll be able to work tomorrow. I wonder how she did it. It's a bad stage to work on; it slopes.

EDITOR'S NOTE: I remember my mother telling me that when she and Betty danced on the London Palladium stage, it was the most difficult stage they ever danced on because the stage sloped down from back to front in order for the audience to see the performers' feet better.

Had to work alone today. Betts can't even walk. Mother took her to the doctor and he gave her a good electric treatment and massage and baked her. Poor kid. All her muscles are torn and they bled internally. She'll have to lay off for several days. The sloping stage could have caused it. It is so hard to work alone. I've got to get used to it. But it's difficult to dance on a slope.

EDITOR'S NOTE: I remember my mother telling me that when she and Betty were dancing at the London Palladium, one of their dances was a tap dance that they did in a large sandbox with sand in it. Just enough sand in the bottom of the box, so when they danced vigorously, with tap shoes, the sand would fly up all around them, and that was quite a spectacle to watch! However, she said it was one of the hardest dances they ever did, especially on the sloping London Palladium stage!

Betts seems a little better today, but she still is flat on her back. No shows on Sunday, which is a good thing because I would have to work alone anyway.

Elinor working alone again.....

I was so mad today. This starts our second week at the Palladium and six new acts came in to take the place of six that closed Saturday night. Betts and I had a darling dressing room on the first floor, but this week they put an opera singer in it, and moved all of our stuff upstairs in a room with four acrobatic girls. A terrible room! So cold and ugly and crowded! The new act is awful. I had to work alone again; Betts cannot walk yet.

Betts is taking treatments every day for her back. I don't know whether she'll be able to work any more this week or not. Poor kid. She has the darndest luck. We decided to go on home with Tom on the 23rd which is a week away. We've had several good offers. Spain, Italy, Egypt, and the Riviera, but will have to wait around a few weeks first, and we can't afford to do that. With Betty in this condition it's best that we go on home. I'm sure we can work better there.

Matinee today. I'm still working alone, and it is so hard on the sloping stage to kick and dance and move around quickly alone without being able to hold onto Betty's shoulder or wrist from time to time to keep ourselves stable. I'm getting beautiful hands from an enthusiastic audience. This is good, if not better than when we're working together. I guess the audience feels sorry for me. The finale is rather hard for me. I have to do my tricks and Betty's too. She seems better today, can walk around a little bit.

Another matinee today which I did alone, the doctor did something today and all of a sudden Betty feels fine. She danced beautifully this evening, although she was a little stiff and her sore muscles pulled a bit. I was more nervous than she. It certainly felt grand having her back again. Jamie Hamilton sent us three mystery books to read on the boat going home.

The prince of Wales was at the last two shows tonight. I'm so glad Betty was there to work with me. He seemed to really enjoy us with a huge smile and heavy applause. Got 13 letters today. Our mail is finally catching up with us from America.

Our last day at the London Palladium. There was so much packing and things to do. I hate to leave such a marvelous audience. There is nothing like it in the states. Bought Ray a Dunhill pipe today. I must see if my money holds out. We were cut $70 on our salary on account of Betty being out for six days. We are always hired as a team, and when Betty is injured, and I have to dance alone, our salary is cut in half. It doesn't really seem fair to us, but that's the way it is.

Got up early and did a little last-minute sightseeing, went to Madame Tussaud's. It is the most famous place of its kind in all the world, all wax works. The Chamber of Horrors wasn't so awful as I thought it would be. Jamie came and took us for a drive to Buckingham Palace, Whitehall, Parliament Law, the mall, and much more. Couldn't see much though because of the heavy, heavy rain.

Spent a very full day on our last day in London. Got up and went down on the mall leading to Buckingham Palace and saw the king open Parliament. So impressive! Then took Betty to the doctor, and from there went to Westminster Abbey. Went all through it and heard the service. It was all very wonderful. Had supper at the Regent Palace, then rushed home to see Jamie who came up to tell us goodbye. Our train for Southampton leaves at 9 AM tomorrow morning.

## *Empress of Britain* in 1931

On our way home at last. This is a beautiful boat, the "Empress of Britain" much larger than the "Paris". We have rooms in tourist class, but we have the run of the entire ship. Quite a lot of people on board. Most of them are taking a world cruise. It must be a wonderful trip. Five entire months cost only $2,000. I'll be glad to get off at New York though. They took two propellers off the boat in order to slow it down for the cruise so it will take seven days to New York instead of 4 1/2.

Just spent a lazy day, did not do much except read and rest. I thought we would get to New York by Sunday night for sure but they're slowing down on purpose so it will be next Wednesday morning before we get in. The sea was pretty smooth today, but it's beginning to get rougher by night. I'm starting to get one of those awful headaches I get from the vibration of the ship.

Oh, Lord, what a day! I wasn't actually seasick, but I never came closer to it in my entire life. It was so rough all day, the ship nearly stood on end. Most everyone was sick. Barbara is pea green. I had lunch in the dining room, but I was afraid to go up for dinner, so I took it in my room. I lay down nearly all day to keep from getting sick. What a horrible feeling.

Felt grand today, nice smooth ocean and I was up and about again. It would take an entire day to explore all of this ship. It surely is a beauty, 42,000 tons. Had cocktails and dinner with some very nice men. Mr. Robbins, who owns the Robbins music publishers in New York. Jimmy Campbell, songwriter, who wrote "Good Night Sweetheart" and many others. And the Paul Whiteman orchestra. Really a good time on this magnificent ship.

Paul Whiteman, leader of one of the most popular dance bands in the United States during the 1920s and 1930s.

Our last day at sea. This is certainly been a long drawn out trip. Packed our trunk and bags and we got in at quarantine at 10 PM tonight, but don't dock in New York till about 10 tomorrow morning. Hope Daddy got our cable all right and will be there to meet us. I wonder if Ray will meet me. I wrote him but didn't cable him.

Gee, it's good to be home again, Daddy and several others met us at the ship, but I was disappointed that Ray wasn't there, but I phoned him when I got home, and he had no definite word from me so he had no way of knowing when I would be home. I cannot wait to see him tomorrow, I love him so.

Me and my Ray

Ray came over at 1 PM. I was so glad to see him. Clem, the boy I went around with in Paris, and London came home a week before I did. He lives in Philadelphia so today he came clear to New York to see me. I was glad to see him again, but I was bored and kept wishing he'd go home. Took a drive with him and he has a nice Buick convertible roadster. He went back to Philly at 7 PM. His trip was a waste of time as far as I was concerned. I love Ray.

Went downtown and met Tom and Barbara. We're going to open in Boston Saturday for a week, but we must all work on a cut. Betts and I must take $150 instead of $200 but it will give us a little to keep us going.

In Boston now and we open today and the act is going over great. Had supper tonight with Lou Walters at the Cascades roof, a lovely club on the top floor of the Bradford Hotel. We're going to double there starting Monday, but he's only paying us $90. It helps out the course because we're working on a cut for Tom this week, only getting $150 from him. There's two shows a night at the Cascades 7;30 and 11:30 so we can make them just fine. We can do this!

Oh dear, what a hard day, our first day of doubling at two different locations. Had a little trouble with our music at the club on the first show but the last show was grand and we stopped the show cold with our kick dance! Just do two numbers, that and the pajama dance. We're in the finale too. Good orchestra and a good floor to work on and nice people. All in all this was grand.

Such a perfect happy day, and we came home to see Mrs. Fonker jump out of her window on the 15th floor right next to us and kill herself. She was the wife of an airline pilot. So very sad and we actually saw it through our window!

Wheeler Twins - Betty + Elinor

Had such a good time tonight. It was theatrical night at the Cascades and it was packed. There were loads of stars and important people there. Our pajama dance stopped the show cold tonight and I was so glad, because it was the first time Tom had seen it. We stayed and danced after the show and got home at 3 AM.

I feel dead tired all day, could hardly work. The strain of doubling in two different places is beginning to be felt.

Got in New York at 7:30 AM, dead tired. Didn't sleep a wink on the train last night. Slept all day and then went down to the casino theater and gave an audition for the new George White Varieties. Tom saw the whole act, and he really liked it and he's going to use us for sure. I'm so tickled. It means we cannot go to Florida this year but I don't care.

I had a lot of fun today. Met Ray at 34th St. at 2:30 and took him back up to the casino with me while I spoke to Tom about rehearsal. Then we went to see a friend of his. Captain Paradine, who runs the boat to the Statue of Liberty. He took us over and we climbed to the very top. Some climb. Went back to Jersey for dinner and then home .

Today is Christmas day and very hot and muggy. I stayed in Jersey City all night. The party at Ray's broke up so late that I had Mrs. Nichols call Mother and tell her I wouldn't be home. Went over to Joe's house first, who is Ray's married brother, an eye doctor, and helped trim their tree and fill the children's stockings. Then back to Ray's house to trim their tree. Had quite a party. Ray gave me an exquisite Waterman Lady Patricia fountain pen and pencil set. Made of pearl. So lovely.

Ray came over tonight and we went out for a long drive and had a very long talk and came to a better understanding about ourselves. He is the dearest thing. I surely love him.

This is December 31 of 1932. This has been a funny year for me. I seem to have gone through so many moods. As I read back through this book, I can't understand how I could have been so infatuated with Freddie. Now I find I hardly even think of him, and I am already and sincerely in love with Ray. But Ray and I are just beginning to understand each other. While I was away from him, I didn't think he cared for me. He was so quiet and undemonstrative, and when I met Freddie in Miami, he was so flattering, he seemed to fill something that I missed in Ray. But now that I am home with Ray again, I find I never want to leave him, and even though he is quiet and keeps most of his thoughts to himself, he's sweet and sincere and real and I know he loves me. I'm glad I had that splurge over Freddie and now I'm sure of myself and I'm sure of Ray and I know positively that I love only him. ♥. EDITOR'S NOTE: Thank goodness!!!! Ray is my sweet wonderful dad!) End of 1932

1933

We arrived at Philadelphia today at noon. We were supposed to rehearse but luckily it was called off. We are staying at the St. Francis Hotel, have a nice double room and bath for $12 a week. Trying to save money this trip. Only making $150 and we have to pay out 10%.

Opened at the Jax today. Lovely theater. First show was a mess. Ted forgot the waltz completely but it was perfect by tonight. Four shows. The new pink costumes are stunning. Had a sweet letter from Ray and he phoned me at midnight from Baltimore. So glad to hear from him. Our high kick number is going over great.

Five shows today. The waltz is getting better and better. We love to do it. Have never done a dance like that with a man before.

Mother and Daddy drove over tonight in time to see the 7 o'clock show. We had supper with them and then they stayed for the last show too. It was great to see them but I sure wish Ray could have been along. I have had a letter from him nearly every day. Had to do a benefit tonight after the last show. Betts and I stopped the show cold dancing our "Tea for Two" number. It was grand!

Imaged by Heritage Auctions, HA.com

EDITOR'S NOTE: I was quite excited when I googled Vaudeville and found this print of the Wheeler Twins and discovered that posters of them are still being sold on the Internet!

EDITOR'S NOTE: Not only did the twins mother, (my Nana), design and make all of their costumes, but she was the head of wardrobe for Paramount Studios. An extremely talented costume designer and seamstress, she also designed and painted artwork for Hallmark cards. Shown in the photo with her is not a dance costume, but a costume for a movie star.

We left on the 6:30 train this evening and we got in about 8:00 in the morning in Toronto. I dread next week.

Staying at the Westmoreland Hotel in Toronto, Canada. Lovely and only $10 a week. Four shows today, none tomorrow than three every day.

Got a wire from Mother today saying she had wired Lou Walters about booking us in a club here in Toronto next week. She must be crazy. There aren't any clubs here. Had a darling letter from Ray today. I have a terrible cold. Got my feet wet, I guess. Too cold and too much snow.

Started getting a new routine today. Alberto de Lima is giving it to us, a semi-classical modernistic number to "Manhattan Serenade ". Something entirely different from our usual stuff, but the public seems to want something different. Paying $7.50 an hour for it. Must get it in two or three lessons. Nice letter from Nickie today.

EDITOR'S NOTE:

My mother nicknamed Ray "Nickie"because it kind of sounds like his last name, Nichols. Several years later, Ray told her that he didn't care for that name, and that if she did not quit calling him Nickie, he would start calling her Mickie! That name stuck, and she was Mickie for her entire life... And it really suited her!

Took another lesson from Alberto today. We have to finish the dance tomorrow. Can't afford to take any more. Had a card from an agent who wants to put us in a big act, but he only pays $150. Wouldn't take it. Feel awful tonight. My cold is worse.

Finished our dance today. It's very rough so we must spend several weeks practicing and perfecting it before we can use it any place. Bitterly cold today, the coldest day we've had. Phoned Ray's mother tonight. She invited me out to supper and I would love to go. I always enjoy myself over there. Had a grand letter from Ray tonight. He's hardly missed a day writing since he's been away. I surely miss my sweet man.

Had a Valentine from Ray today, I knew I'd get one. Had a darling letter from him too. Sent a wire to Ray Teal yesterday asking him if he could book us in Miami. Had an answer from him tonight saying he could give us three days at the Olympia Theater in Miami at $75 so we're starting Saturday. Going to drive down in Madame Queen, our Chevy. So happy!

EDITOR'S NOTE: Olympia Theater, (on left side of street, vertical marquee) built in 1926 as a silent movie palace. It was the first air-conditioned building in the south. It served as a concert hall, movie theater and performing arts center and had a capacity of 2,170 people. (It is still a grand venue today).

We are so busy all day dashing around downtown doing last minute things. Bought some white shoes for Miami and it seems so funny while everyone here is slapping around in galoshes. Got our trunk all packed and it goes out tomorrow. Have to send it by boat. A friend of Daddy's is going to drive down with us most of the way. We have to save ourselves, so we'll be able to start work Thursday. Mother is going too. Sent Ray a wire letting him know.

I'll be so glad to get away, especially to Florida. I need some new clothes so badly but can't afford to get a thing. Hope Ray can get down while I'm there. I'll just die if he can't.

Made Richmond Virginia tonight, 353 miles. Stopped at Fredericksburg for dinner at 6 PM then decided to drive onto Richmond. Got here at 8:45.

On our way again at 7:30 AM. Had bright sunshine so far, hope it keeps up. Made 526 miles today, from Richmond to Savannah, Georgia. Switched off Route 1 at Raleigh and took 401, much shorter.

Could have made Miami by tonight if we had wanted to push it, but we didn't want to get in so late and have to look for some place to stay. So we slept late this morning and didn't start until 10:00. Took it easy all day, but managed to do 400 miles stopping at Fort Pierce, Florida for the night.

Arrived in Miami at 11 AM. Took us until 4 PM to find a place to stay. This place is certainly flooded this season. There isn't a single vacancy on the beach, and the hotel rates are enormous. Finally found a room in a beautiful private home in Miami, 221 N. E. 21st St., only $18 a week. We may not stay longer than a week, so we can't take a place for a month. Certainly is hot here. I am so tickled to be back again.

Went to the Olympia Theater and saw the show, very good. Sally Rand was in it. Went to see Billy Dozier last night, and the darn thing is married now, only 21 years old. Got married in December to some girl he met in North Carolina. She seems all right, but I only saw her in the dark.

Opened at the Olympia today, and we went over great. We do two numbers, "Tea for Two" and "Harlem Moon". Three shows a day. We're going to double at the Floridian Hotel Saturday and Sunday so that means $50 extra. So hot here, hope to get a good tan before I leave.

Dancing at the Olympia Theater in Miami, a happy place for us. Also dancing at the Biltmore Hotel and Roney Plaza this month, busy time!

After the second show today, one of the musicians came up to my dressing room and told me there was a young man to see me. So I went down, and there was Ray! I was so surprised and happy. He really wasn't supposed to get here until Sunday, two days from now. He took me to dinner, and I saw him after the last show. It surely is grand having him down here with me.

Danced at the Biltmore tonight, and it was a mess! The orchestra was awful, and played one number too fast and the other too slow. The floor was so slippery I almost fell, and managed to hurt my back and shoulder. Had a good time afterward though. Steve Gibbs and his wife were there and of course my Ray. Poured rain but the place was really crowded and grand applause.

We moved today and found an apartment we could take by the week, 242 N. E. 32nd St. in Miami. We decided to leave the 18th of this month with Ray Teal to play eight weeks in North and South Carolina and Virginia. He wanted us to go to Nassau with him this Saturday but we have had some stuff booked here and thought we better stay. So cold today we had to wear coats.

Had a card and a letter from Ray today. He will get back tomorrow afternoon. Danced at the Roney Plaza tonight, did two numbers. Tiny floor and a bad orchestra, but we went over fine.

Moved again today to a darling little apartment in Coral Gables, only $20 a month and it has five rooms and a bathroom. It's quite a long way out here from Miami Beach but it's quiet and so pretty, and we're away from the noisy tourists. The address is 222 Avenue Colabria. Danced again tonight at Flamingo Park and got another check. Hope we can cash them soon as we only have about nine dollars in ready cash left.

Flamingo Hotel at the 36 acre Flamingo Park in Miami Beach, Florida.

Another scrumptious day. Washed my hair, so it would look nice for tonight. Danced at the Roney Plaza, the big charity ball in the gardens. It was a benefit so we weren't paid. We're going to work at the Roney all next week.

Getting a grand tan by going to the beach every opportunity. Started working at the Roney Plaza tonight. We get room and board free and all the privileges of the place, but no salary. It will be a nice week for us, though, right here on the beach, and everything is very spiffy and ritzy. Mother will stay out in Coral Gables in the apartment, but we'll run out to see her every day or so. Only one show at night, at 9 PM. So easy.

Elinor, mother Wilna, and Betty.

Got up early and went out on the beach for a couple of hours. It's grand to be right here at the Roney and practically stepped right into the ocean for a swim. Drove out to see Mother this afternoon in Coral Gables. Had a lot of mail at the apartment. Ray hasn't had any of my letters yet. They must have just missed him. Poor kid. Blazing hot all day. Getting a great tan.

Blazing hot again today. The publicity photographer at the hotel here took a lot of photos of us in our bathing suits. We'll see them tomorrow morning.

Roney Plaza Hotel. 1930's

Saw our pictures this morning. They're very good and we wanted some but they're a dollar each, so that's out. We are loving the Roney Plaza and will hate to leave here when we finish next week. Everything has been so lovely. Coral Gables is so far out and it's so hard to get in to the beach.

We opened at the Olympia Theater today. We played there just three weeks ago. This is "Appreciation Week". All the big acts from expensive clubs are performing in this grand theater. We are one of the headliners. They kicked about our tan so we have to use whitening. We double between here and the Roney Plaza.

I don't know when I've been so tired. Did three shows at the Olympia and two at the Roney Plaza. They want us to work here at the Roney next week, but I don't think we will. We don't get anything out of it and it is too hard to double. Had a nice letter from Ray today. Mother came over and is staying with us all night.

Four shows at the Olympia today, so we didn't have time to do the one at the Roney. Awfully tired. Working in this heat wears you out. We're through at the theater tomorrow night. A new show goes in on Tuesday.

Downtown Miami in 1933

Supposed to dance out at the Biltmore Hotel pools this afternoon, but we had floods of rain all day, so the whole show was called off.

Stayed on the beach about three hours and got a good burn. Had a sweet letter from Ray. Made me blue and homesick for him.

I received a letter from Ray today, such a darling letter. Today is his birthday (March 28) and I'm so lonesome. I couldn't send him anything, no money.

A gorgeous sunny day today. Performed at the show at the Biltmore pool today. Did one number and got $15 for it. Mother baked a lemon icebox pie for us tonight and it was so good.

Poured rain all day. Stayed home and did jigsaw puzzles. Had three grand letters and a card from my Nickie today. He's in Tennessee now and they are going on home. Expect to be there by next Sunday. Wish I could go home. We're going straight to Chicago from here in about a month. Want so much to see Ray but I won't see him for so long.

Went deep-sea fishing with Jimmy today. There were eight of us all together. I was the only one who caught anything, landed a 10 pound tuna. Such a thrill, the first time I've ever been fishing. Had it dressed and divided it with Jimmy and Carl. Had it for supper tonight and it was surely good. Had another sweet letter from Ray.

Today, we all went out to the Pan-American flying field to watch the big clipper ships land. So thrilling. They certainly are immense things. Didn't go out tonight.

Pan American Airways 1930's clipper ship

Mother, Betts and I went downtown today. Rented a machine so we could dig in and do a lot of sewing. Started a little white and yellow dress. Hope to get it done in a couple of days. Had a sweet letter from Nickie today.

Stayed in all day and sewed. My dress is all finished now, except putting on the snaps. It is so cute, white trimmed in yellow. Wish I had some extra money. There are some marvelous sales every place now.

Got a letter from Daddy and he sounded homesick so Mother has about made up her mind to go home next week. I certainly hope we do. We have two weeks in New York before we have to leave for Chicago.

Started for New York today. Got off at 7 AM, but discovered a bad knock in the engine, so stopped in at the Firestone place. A whole new gear wheel had to be put in and we had to wait until 1 PM. Too bad, but it was a good thing we discovered it before we had a breakdown on the road. Couldn't get far today, getting such a late start. Stopped for the night just south of Titusville, Florida, in the Bayview Hotel. Car is running great. We are keeping it down to about 40 miles an hour.

Bayview Hotel located on US 1 in Titusville, Florida, was built in the late 1800s.

*Col. Henry T. Titus (1823-1881)*

Colonel Henry Titus, founded the city of Titusville in 1869.

EDITOR'S NOTE: My husband, Bob, Kirk, with our two children, Robby and Cathy, moved to Titusville in 1967. Krista was born there in 1974, and we lived there through the early 90's. My two older children live there to this day with their families. I was elected the first woman president of the Titusville Chamber of Commerce and also the first woman to ever serve on a bank board in Brevard county and was presented with several other county-wide awards... I loved living and raising my children there, 11 years of the 24 years as a single mom.

Lew Wolfe from the Paris office of the William Morris office, called us and wanted to know if we would sail for Paris Saturday to open at the Ambassadeurs. We won't go unless they'll pay us $250 and passage both ways, so he's cabling and we're waiting to hear. It would be nice as it's only a four week job and we could get back in time to go to Chicago for the World's Fair. I saw my Nickie tonight.

Well, the Paris thing is all off, and I am glad. With the US off the gold standard now, you can't tell what they're going to do with salaries. It is all for the best, we can relax a little before our big opening in Chicago.

Well, the Chicago opening was quite a success although of course we were all nervous. Quite a good crowd, considering that the World's Fair opened today too. Thought I'd get a wire, at least from Nickie, but I guess he forgot. Freddie sent me four dozen beautiful tea rose buds. I was so thrilled.

Had a letter from Nickie today and he sent me three lovely purses, so sweet of him.

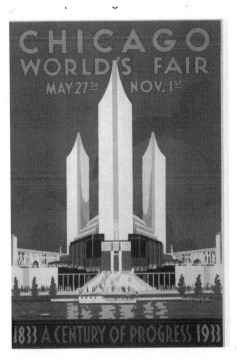

EDITOR'S NOTE: The 1933 World's Fair, introduced many new things, including elevators, the zipper, Cracker Jacks, the Ferris wheel, and more.

Had a grand crowd tonight. Had to do three shows for the first time since we've opened. Our pictures are in today's Americas, a big two column picture. Very nice.

New York

Our pictures were supposed to be in today's Herald Examiner, but they weren't. Johnny says they'll be in next Sunday. Had good business tonight although it rained like the dickens. The floor was so slippery we could hardly work. Everyone fell. It was awful. The audience noticed, and from time to time we could hear little gasps from different people in the audience. As they say, "the show must go on! ". Something fun to talk about later, and no one was hurt.

Scorching day. Hope this heat makes me lose a little weight. What with exercising and dieting, it shouldn't take long. I'm 117, and want to get down to 112 or 110. Every time I gain an ounce, I get it in my thighs. Had a sweet letter from Nickie. He's in Kentucky now. He'll get here in about three weeks. Can hardly wait to see him.

Started to learn our new dance today. It's for the opening revolutionary number, a torch dance. A lot of running and leaping. Not much to it, but we've never done that sort of thing before so it seems awkward. The rest of the people in the show are here now.

Another sweet letter from my Nickie. So stiff today from that crazy dance. Learned some more of it. Freddie was here today with his orchestra to give an audition for Bouche'. He has a grand band, but I think Boo is going to take Saunders band instead.

Didn't do much today except rehearse a little. Can't do much. We're too stiff. More rehearsing, more rehearsing. We've got the whole dance now. But it's very rough. Will have to practice it hard.

Rehearsed quite a few hours this afternoon. The orchestra started rehearsing the show music today. I guess will have to put in some really hard work this next week.

Same old thing day after day, just sit around and wait your turn to rehearse. If it wasn't for Nickie's letters every day, I don't know what I'd do.

Rehearsed until midnight. I'll be so glad when we open Saturday night and really get started on the job. Have a dandy band. Coon and Saunders, old band. The band leaders name is Frankie Martel.

The Wheeler Twins

Well, the opening was quite a success, although, of course, we were all nervous. Quite a good crowd, considering that the World's Fair opens today.

Had quite a wind storm today, so it cooled things off a lot. Had to even wear a coat tonight. Had a marvelous crowd at all the shows.

There was a terrible airplane crash near here today. A plane from the World's Fair with nine passengers crashed and caught fire. All of them killed. June 12, 1933.

The New York Times

SUBSCRIBE FOR $1/WEEK

## CHICAGO FAIR PLANE KILLS NINE IN CRASH; At Least 3 New Yorkers Are Among 7 Passengers Perishing in Flames. CAUGHT IN SUDDEN SQUALL Pontoon Smashes on Lake and on Re-Ascent, Crumpling Wing Causes Plunge. CHICAGO FAIR PLANE KILLS 9 IN CRASH

Got into lo Chicago about 4:30 this afternoon and it was surely a rotten trip. The roads were torn up all the way. We don't start work for three more days so we can get upacked and.settled in.

We had a nice time today. Drove down to the Drake to step off our routines on the floor. Then we drove to the Villa. We saw Mr. Bouche' and he had his usual grouch on.

Image taken from www.TheDrakeHotel.com

### The Drake Hotel in Culture and Literature

The Drake Hotel's rich history and association with all things Chicago mirrors the realist style found within the majority of the works we read in English 280 throughout the semester. The Drake Hotel watched on as Chicago hosted The World's Fair, dealt with prohibition and Al Capone, and has made cameo appearances in popular culture and literature.

Went to rehearsal this afternoon and went over our music with the band. There's a grand band here at the Drake, but there's not a violin, and we really need them in our dances. Opened tonight and there was not a huge crowd there, but it was Monday night. We did three shows though, 8:30, 10, and 12 midnight.

Had really good shows tonight, quite a good crowd. Freddie called me at the Drake. He was at the World's Fair with his mother and had been there since noon. He must have been plenty tired. He has to work tomorrow but I may see him after the job.

Betts and I drove downtown today and bought a record and an orchestration of "Mood Indigo ". We're going to put a new dance in Monday and we decided to get up something easy to fit our new music. So we borrowed a Victrola and practiced all afternoon, and made up a really cute dance.

There's a rhythm in Victor dance music that brings joy with every step

And no wonder! The best dance orchestras make Victor Records—Paul Whiteman and His Orchestra, The Benson Orchestra of Chicago, Club Royal Orchestra, Joseph C. Smith and His Orchestra, The Virginians, All Star Trio and Their Orchestra, Hackel-Berge Orchestra, International Novelty Orchestra, and other favorite organizations. And such records played as only the Victrola can play them make dance music a perpetual delight. Victrolas in great variety of styles from $25 to $1500.

"HIS MASTER'S VOICE" **Victrola**

Important: Look for these trade-marks. Under the lid. On the label. Victor Talking Machine Company, Camden, New Jersey

Went down to the Drake at 2 PM and rehearsed our new music with the orchestra. It was the only time they could give us. Then we went over to see Priscilla and she went over our music on the piano so we could see if it would fit. Pretty good shows tonight. Freddie met me after the last show and we had something to eat.

Went swimming with Freddie today. Didn't go till late so I didn't get sunburned. Went to a beach way up north in no man's land. Had a dandy time. We came back here to dress and then he took me out to supper. Got home early, about 12:30.

Put a new dance in the show tonight, our "Mood Indigo" number. It went over fine. The costumes are so pretty, chartreuse satin with gold beaded tops, and the skirt is split way above the knee over one leg.

Got a good baking on the roof today. I'm surely getting a dandy tan, but it's hard to keep unless I go after it every day. I want to be able to go home to New York with some tan. Ray called me today. I am so homesick for him.

Much cooler today. The awful heat finally broke. Started to make a new dress, white organdy with eyelet embroidery. It's going to be a semi-formal dress, very long with a ruffle around the bottom and very low in the back. Sewed on it all day. Have no machine so I have to do it all by hand.

We intend to leave for New York in a few days so I got some last minute things attended to. Had the radio in the car fixed, cost me $4.50. Bought a jack for the car, the last one we had got lost. Had another good time tonight. Freddie came for me about 6 and we celebrated with a last good time in Chicago. Had supper downtown and then went to a movie and saw a peachy show.

I'm going down to the shore with Ray over the weekend. His family has a cottage at Belmar Beach, so we're going down Friday evening and stay through Sunday. So I had to go downtown today and buy some shoes to go with my new white organdy dress.

Had a long hard day today, rehearsals from noon until after 6:00 then again from 8:00 till 10. Ray called me and we went up to Bob Hauser's place on 92nd St. and Broadway but I was so tired I could not enjoy myself.

The costumer came in today and took orders for the costumes. Our things are all furnished, so that's one big saving. Betts and I get five changes, an afternoon dress, sport dress, cheerleader's outfit, evening dress, and a Dutch costume. I think we have more than anyone else in the show.

Had to rehearse late again tonight. We start at noon every day and end up after six and sometimes we have to go back after supper and rehearse until 10. The show is shaping up fine. I think it is going to be a peach. Saw the sketches for our costumes and they're simply beautiful.

Such a beautiful day. Especially after yesterday's rain. We had to rehearse from 12 until 4 and I was so mad because I wanted to go down to Belmar with Ray. He had to go down today to bring his family home. They have been there for five weeks and the season is over now.

Good crowd tonight, and we only had to do two shows. The young gardener here where we live, 22 years old, was hit by a car out in the road tonight and he is not expected to live. Fractured his skull.

A Buick man from Evanston sent out two cars for us to look at today, a 1930 Pontiac, which we weren't interested in and a 1932 Ford which is a dandy. We're going to trade in our old car for a newer one.

Looked at another car today, a 32 V8 Ford in beautiful condition. It's only gone 2300 miles. I think we may get it. Only $320 with our car.

A dandy crowd tonight, quite amazing for a Monday night. We went to see about the car today and we have decided to buy it. Tested it for gas and oil consumption all afternoon. It gets about 16 or 18 miles on the gallon. Not bad for eight cylinders. Going to get it on Thursday.

Went to get our new car today, but we couldn't take it out unless we paid cash for it. He forgot to send in a statement about us taking it out on payments. We will get it next week.

We rather thought Daddy would pop in on us tonight as he said last week he had a surprise for us. We had a hunch he was coming to see us, but I guess we were wrong. Haven't heard from him for several days so we thought he was on the way. Good crowd tonight.

Jane and Billy had a fit today when they were told they weren't needed any more. They thought they were the biggest stars in the show and they would last longer than anyone else. But they surely got fooled. The show is all different now. Victor took the best numbers out of each show and combined them into one. It makes a great show. We give the same one twice a night.

Thankfully, we have never been let go from any show... Although people all around us seem to have bad luck sometimes.

We have to give an audition tomorrow for the Congress Hotel. Wish we could work there. It's the spiffiest place in all of Chicago. Had a letter from Nickie today and one from Freddie. Hear from Nickie every day.

We gave an audition today for Mr. Kaufman and Mr. Robinson, who run the Congress Hotel. They liked us very much, but weren't willing to pay the salary we asked. He may come up a little though. Mother is going to phone him tomorrow morning.

Saw Freddie a while this afternoon. He had to leave early to be at his broadcast downtown so he had to bring me home at 3:30. Just had time to have a little beer together. I told him to sing a song for me on the air tonight, so I listened in on his Broadcast. He sang "Thanks For the Memory" for me and even mentioned my name. I was so tickled.

The twins' dad Harry Wheeler having fun!

We are so excited. Had a letter from Daddy and he's coming here to Chicago! Firestone Tire and Rubber Company, is sending its five best men here for a week, all expenses paid. He gets here Sunday, so we dashed right out and found a cute apartment on the northside. We close at the Villa tomorrow night so we can't stay on here. Thank goodness!

Villa Venice ballroom and stage

I'm so fed up with the place where we are staying. Our trunks have to go out tomorrow morning so we have a lot of packing to do tonight.

The trunks went out today and we got all the rest of the packing done. Going to move into Chicago tomorrow morning early, so will be there when Daddy calls at noon. Can hardly wait to see him. Our last night at the Villa. It's been a long tremendous run all right although the reviews have been tremendous.

## Villa Venice Stages Smart Revue of Beauty Unadorned by Fig Leaves.

### By Frederic Babcock.

THE lights grow dim, the curtains part, and eight figures insinuate themselves out across the floor. They raise flaming torches. They dance. They are no pony ballet, cute, cuddlesome, with fixed smiles painted on tired faces. They are tall, lithesome, serious, self-contained. This is serious business. It's la Danse de la Revolution.

*The mob of eight slinks back into obscurity and is replaced by its leaders. They are the Wheeler twins. They dance for the joy of dancing. They personify youth. They have the freedom and the abandon of real artistry. They apply the torch; the crowd is set aflame.*

Moved to the new apartment this morning. It's surely nice. Daddy got here about 12:20 and we were so tickled to see him. He decided to stay here with us instead of at a hotel with the rest of the men. We all drove to the Villa this afternoon to get our money, last week's salary and the first week he held out on everyone. So we got $250. Johnny came to the apartment this evening and we all went to the Italian restaurant at the fair. Freddie is in the orchestra there and we all had a glorious time.

Went to the fair today with Daddy. Today was Firestone Day there, and what a mob of men! We met a lot of the men from Daddy's office. Then the three of us took in a few of the sites. Went to Ripley's. He surely has some queer things in there. Didn't leave there till 5:30 PM and we were surely dead when we got home. Johnny came up to the apartment and brought us a little radio. So nice of him. We wanted one so badly.

Got our new car today and paid the balance due on it, $183. Really hated to see the last of Madame Queen, our red Chevy, but she was really worn out. The new one we have, a Ford coach V8 is grand, it drives like a dream. October 10, 1933.

The twins' new Ford Coach V-8

Gave an audition today for the College Inn downtown. They liked us very much and we may go in on Monday. If not, we'll go to Detroit.

Grandfather got here today from Indianapolis. He's going to stay with us for a week. Daddy left for New York tonight. Surely hated to see him go. It was so grand having him here with us. I wanted to go back with him, I am so homesick for Ray.

Grandfather Warden Booth English

Expected to open at the College Inn tonight, but they couldn't get the musicians together for a rehearsal, so we'll open tomorrow night.

We opened at the College Inn tonight, and we were a terrible flop. Can't understand why at least one of our numbers didn't go big, but they didn't seem to like it at all. Guess they won't keep us long. I don't know what kind of crowd this is or what they expect.

Went to Maurice, the photographer today to get some photos we ordered and I had them take a few heads of me. Ray wants a new picture. I'll see the proofs Monday. The College Inn was certainly jammed tonight and it was pouring rain too. We put a new number in our act, Manhattan Serenade. It went over way better than we expected.

Went to see my proofs today, and I was rather disappointed in them. The one I thought would be good didn't turn out at all well. One of the serious ones was very good though, so I took that one. I had one big one made to send to Ray and three small ones. Got very good hands tonight at the show; this place surely does good business.

Got my picture that Maurice took of me, the big one came out lovely. Mailed it to Ray. Hope he likes it. Freddie came to the College Inn tonight and saw the first show. Then I went out with him.

Met Freddie at 1 o'clock and spent the afternoon with him. Had to do an extra performance tonight at the Knickerbocker Hotel for the Chicago Times. Didn't get paid but we're supposed to get some great publicity out of it.

Had a photo in today's news and a picture and write up in "This Week in Chicago". Hurt my knee last night, so went to the doctor today. Pulled a ligament.

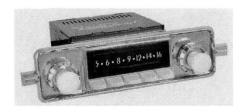

1933 car radio

Johnny had a radio put in our car for us. He certainly has given us a lot. Had to do an extra show tonight. It was fine, great audience.

Had a cute write-up in today's Herald Examiner, a whole column. Didn't go out of the hotel all day. Stayed in and rested. Our two weeks will be up Tuesday and I will be glad to leave, resting my bad knee.

Freddie opened tonight at the Canton Tea Garden. I wanted to go to the opening but we had to go to the Chez Paree.

Met Freddie downtown tonight at the Canton Tea Garden and had supper with him. He had from 8 to 10 off so I only had two hours with him. Getting awfully cold again here, but it is November. Wish the warm weather would keep up.

Rainy night so we didn't have as much of a crowd as we expected. Only had to do two shows. I started a new book at 6 PM and finished it about midnight. Read between dances and every minute I possibly could. It was so exciting I could hardly put it down. "Brood of the Witch Queen" by Saks Rohmer.

EDITOR'S NOTE; I thought it would be interesting to Google this book to see if I could find it, because my mother found it so extremely fascinating. Luckily, I found it and purchased on

Amazon! (Not really my style though, I am not into science fiction)

Bea Becker from New York called me up today. She and another girl from Canada hitchhiked here to see the Worlds Fair. They're going back in a few days. They certainly have a lot of nerve to undertake a trip like that. Imagine what could happen to them, hitchhiking all that way! She might come out to see the show Friday night

Certainly had a tremendous crowd tonight. Every table was taken by 9:30 PM and they turned them away by the dozens all evening. Drove into Chicago this afternoon to see Esther Crawford. Had an early supper with her, then brought her back out here with us to see the show. She enjoyed it so much.

Ray's birthday gift came to me tonight and it's a lovely folding camera. Something I have always wanted. I am so tickled with it. I cannot wait to go take photos with it and see how they come out.

1930's folding camera

Had to take Betty to the doctor today. She hurt her knee last night and could hardly walk. When she got up today, it was very bad. One of the bones was out of place and it had to be set back in. The doctor wanted to put it in a splint, but she had to dance, so he just taped it. She got along fine in the shows.

Spent the afternoon with Freddie today. Had a lovely time. Mother and Betts did some shopping today and got me a cute white rubber bathing suit with a skirt to match. Betty got a blue one. Had a big lovely crowd tonight. We've been very lucky the last few nights with large crowds.

Two grand letters from Nickie and a big box of salt water taffy today. So sweet of him. Took it downtown in the dressing room to share with all the girls, and the whole 2 pounds disappeared in a flash. Marvelous crowd tonight. Had three shows. A new prima donna went in last night. She's not so good.

Slept till 5 PM. Nothing to do on Sundays but rest. Can't even go to the post office. Had another picture in today's Tribune. It was really grand, a huge one too, four columns wide. A nice write up too. Jane and Billy were so jealous. They went to Bouche' about it, and he told them to go to hell. Nice crowd tonight and we only had to do two shows.

Nize, Nicht?

THE WHEELER TWINS, who are among the headliners of the Jack Venice show. Chicago

Another month started. Hope this month goes very fast. I'm getting so homesick for Ray I can hardly stand it. In his letter today, he said the whole family is going down to the shore over the holiday weekend for Labor Day. If I was there, I could have such a good time.

Had a glorious day. Went to the air races today. They started at one and lasted till seven. It was so wonderful. One thing spoiled the day though. The one woman pilot in the last race, lost the wing fabric from her plane and crashed to death. She was killed instantly, and only 26 years old.

Mother had her hair bobbed and a permanent wave today. It looks grand. No letter from Nickie today. Felt so homesick. I'm getting awfully fed up with this place and I want to go home.

Wilna, the twins' mother, professional seamstress and manager as well as an artist for Hallmark cards.

Got another big box of candy from Nickie today and a sweet letter. Grand crowd tonight but a little too noisy. Everyone in the cast seems so tired. This was our 15th week of work.

A gorgeous day. So bright and sunny, but cool. Took a little drive by myself, felt kinda lonesome. Washed my hair and wrote some letters. Good crowd tonight. The young gardener here, 22 years old, was hit by a car out in the road tonight and he's not expected to live, fractured his skull.

Had to take the car to the Chevrolet place today to get the battery recharged. Couldn't start it this morning. Had to push it all around the drive to get it going. We are going to try and trade it in on another one. I'm afraid it will not get us home over the mountains.

We went to get the battery fixed on the car, but it couldn't be charged because one of the cells was dead. So we have to buy a new one. Looked around at some good 1932 used cars. We've decided to trade ours in. Had two nice letters from Nickie today.

Saw Freddie a while this afternoon. His band is working at the fair now. Mr. Fitzgibbons, a Buick man sent out two cars for us to look at today, a 1930 Pontiac, which we we're not interested in and a 1932 Ford which is a dandy. We're going to trade in our old car on a newer one.

Looked at another car today, a 1932 V8 Ford coach, in beautiful condition. It's only gone 2300 miles. I think we may get it. Only $3200 with our old car.

Pouring rain tonight, so there was not a huge crowd during the shows. Actually, we only had to do one show tonight, that's the first time anything like that has ever happened. We drove to Evanston today in the pouring rain but it was fun. Had to keep the car going to keep it from drowning.

We went to get our new car today, but we couldn't take it out unless we paid cash. He forgot to send in a statement about us taking it out on payments. I guess we'll get it next week.

EDITOR'S NOTE: Aways beautifully dressed, notice her gloves.

Mother went into Chicago today to see some agents about some work for us. We close at the end of the week so we want to get a few extra weeks in before we go home. We have to give an audition tomorrow for the Congress Hotel. Wish we could work there. It is the spiffiest place in all of Chicago. I hear from Nicki every day.

Saw Freddie awhile this afternoon. He had to leave early to be at his broadcast downtown so he had to bring me home at 3:30. Just had time to have a little beer together. I told him to sing a song for me on the air tonight so I listened in on his broadcast. He sang "Thanks for the Memory" for me and even mentioned my name. I was so tickled.

Twins' dad, Harry Beech Wheeler.

We're so excited. Had a letter from Daddy and he's coming here to Chicago! Firestone is sending its five best men here for a week, all expenses paid. He gets here Sunday. So we dashed right out and found a cute apartment on the northside. We close at the Villa tomorrow night so we can't stay on here. Thank goodness.

I'm so fed up with the shows. Our trunks have to go out tomorrow morning so we have a lot of packing to do tonight.

Moved to the new apartment this morning, it's surely nice. Daddy got here about 12 today and we are so tickled to see him. He decided to stay here with us instead of at a hotel with the rest of the men. We all drove out to the Villa this afternoon to get our money from last week's salary and the first week he held out on everyone, so we get $250.

They loved our audition for the College Inn; we got the job! We expected to open tonight, but they couldn't get the musicians together for a rehearsal in time, so we'll open tomorrow night.

EDITOR'S NOTE: The College Inn in the Hotel Sherman was one of Chicago's premier night spots in the 20's and 30's with bandleader Isham Jones, who made it a jazz venue. Before that, hotels featured only genteel string orchestras. The College Inn was not integrated and had an all-white jazz orchestra.

Isham Jones. Famous jazz musician and orchestra leader.

We opened at the College Inn tonight, and we were a terrible flop. Can't understand why at least one of our numbers didn't go big, but they didn't seem to click at all. Guess they won't keep us long. Let's just hope for the best! It might have just been an off-night for the audience.

Our music was much better tonight, except for "Tea for Two" and that was too fast. We ended up, quite breathless!

Palace Theater    N.Y.                            12 - '34

Went out with Freddie this afternoon. Had a lovely time. The shows were fine tonight. We don't go over as well here as we did at Bouche's but I guess it's good enough. Maybe it is a more sophisticated and subdued audience.

A new team went into the show tonight, a comedy, dance trio, and they are certainly good. We put in a new number in our Manhattan Serenade. It went over better than we expected, quite great.

Met Freddie at 1 o'clock and spent the afternoon with him. Had to do an extra performance tonight at the Knickerbocker Hotel for the Chicago Times. Didn't get paid but we are supposed to get some publicity out of it.

Had a picture in today's news and also a picture and write up in "This Week in Chicago". Hurt my knee last night, so went to the doctor today. Pulled a ligament. Keep it warm and wrapped tomorrow for sure so I can dance without any problems tomorrow night.

Johnny had a radio put in our car for us. He certainly has given us a lot. He has been such a dear friend to us, and really genuine. Had to do an extra show tonight.

We had a wire from Max Richard saying he could book us in Akron and Youngstown for one week at $225. We wired back an OK and decided to leave for New York Saturday morning. Tonight an offer came through for four weeks at the Forest Club in New

Orleans at $250 a week and we couldn't take it because we had already taken the other job. I want to go home to New York anyway.

Our last day in Chicago. I'll be glad to leave here. It was just six months ago that we left New York. Had dinner tonight with Freddie and his mother. Hope I see him soon again.

We got started at seven this morning. At South Bend we ran into snow and ice and from there all the roads were awful. This trip should be made in two days but if we don't run out of the snow, it's going to be slow going. We just got a little beyond Cleveland tonight, bad icy roads.

What a day, we're all on the verge of insanity! The roads were covered with ice and slush all the way, and we didn't average over 20 miles an hour, just kept skidding and sliding all over the place. Only made 200 miles all day long today. Had to stop at 6 o'clock, couldn't keep on. The poor car is a mess, covered with mud and ice.

Ran out of snow finally today and we were able to make better time. Got in New York at 5:30 PM and never was I so glad to get to a journey's end. I hope I never have to make another northern trip in the winter. I'm dying to call Ray up, but I can't see him till tomorrow night anyway, so I'll wait and walk in on him and surprise him.

Spent all afternoon downtown doing a little shopping. Bought a coat, dress, two hats and shoes. Got all dolled up tonight, and drove over to see Ray. I walked right in on him, and he nearly fainted with surprise. He grabbed hold of me, and I thought he'd never let me go. His mother wasn't home, but I'll see her in a few days.

Ray and Elinor

Made two platters of fudge today and helped clean house. Drove down to 72nd St. and picked Ray up at 5:30 and then we drove to Jersey and had dinner at his house. His mother was there and I was so glad to see her. About 10 o'clock we went to the Rustic Cabin, a cute place just north of the bridge on the Jersey side where they have a dandy orchestra. I had such a grand time! Danced and danced!

That Akron booking we had was a month from now but we're trying to cancel it because we have to pay our own fares and that amounts to $100. It would be ridiculous to lay out that much money just for one week's work. I haven't heard from Freddie yet. I hope I get a letter soon.

Had quite a good time tonight. Ray took me to a masquerade party out at his cousin's house in Paterson. I wore an old dance costume and Ray wore a clown suit. There were about 20 people there. Going to stay all night at Ray's in Jersey. Too far to go home.

The party at Patterson didn't break up until 4:30 AM this morning and we stopped at another party in Jersey on the way home so didn't get to Ray's until 6:00 AM. Slept till 2 PM and I'm still tired. Ray brought me home and stayed a little while. I caught an awful cold.

I bought two stunning evening dresses, one formal, one semi formal. Both blue, but different shades. I can wear them either here or in Florida. Had a letter from Freddie, the second since I've been home. I surely miss him. He is so sweet.

Thanksgiving Day 1933, stayed home with the family and had a grand dinner. So for that it will take me a week to get over it. We all went to the Audubon tonight and saw a good vaudeville show and two good movies.

Betts and I went with Daddy to the opening broadcast of Firestone tonight. It was a dressy affair and was held at the NBC Studios in Radio City. It only lasted half an hour and seemed rather a waste of time to me. We're all getting ready for tomorrow night. The repeal of prohibition has gone through and the US can have all the liquor it wants. Tomorrow night's the night. Jack, Betts, Ray and myself are going out.

Today is the repeal of prohibition in New York, celebrated as if it were New Year's Eve. Jack, Betts, Ray and I donned evening clothes and went to Ben Riley's. Had a grand time. After we left there, we went down to Jack's house and had some hamburgers. Got home at 5:30 AM.

Found a dandy apartment today and we decided to move into it. Is on Riverside Drive and the whole apartment is being done over and remodeled and it's an awful mess right now but I think it will be ready for us to move in in two weeks. It has four rooms and eight closets, perfect, and only $75 a month. Had dinner in Mount Vernon tonight with Daddy and Eddie and we had a grand time.

Didn't get dressed all day. Washed and polished all the living room furniture and what a job it was. Mother is reupholstering a couple of chairs and everything is in such a mess. We're trying to get all the new drapes and bedspreads for the new apartment made before we move in. Yesterday we bought a lovely new couch and big arm chair. Heard Freddie's broadcast and he mentioned my name.

Had such a grand time tonight. The Saxtons had a big party at their place, 30 people. The biggest party they've ever had. They have the loveliest place to throw a grand party. It didn't break up until 6 AM. Wanted to hear Freddie's broadcast but 1 o'clock just slipped by before I knew it.

Stayed at Ray's last night, it was too late to go home. It was dawn before I got to bed. Slept till 11 AM. Ray brought me home about 3 PM and I got right to work helping Mother and Betts with the sewing. Almost finished the bedspread for our room. It's going to be very elaborate, gold and turquoise.

Put in a full day of sewing today. Didn't even take my pajamas off all day. Got all the curtains for our rooms finished and what a job it was. Six heavy lined drapes, the kind that drag on the floor. It's suddenly turned bitterly cold outside and plenty of snow this first week in December.

Another hard day of work. Betts and I dug in and washed and polished the rest of the furniture, packed the books and pictures and washed all the bric-a-brac. Started the living room curtains. I'm afraid we're not going to be able to finish everything before Monday. So much to do. Heard Freddie's broadcast tonight.

Finished up the living room curtains today. What a job they were. Jack and Ray came over tonight and helped us paint lamps. Had a lot of fun. Ended up by playing poker.

Moved into the new apartment this afternoon and it's going to be lovely. The address is 720 Riverside Dr. at 149th St. in New York City. Got the living room fixed up by tonight and we're all dead tired. Hope we can get it all straightened up here by Christmas which is two weeks from today. We're all crazy about this apartment. It's the nicest one we have ever had.

EDITOR'S NOTE: Whenever an address of a new "cute" apartment was mentioned throughout these diaries, I always googled them for photos, but they are no longer apartment buildings, but huge tall exquisite condominiums! Of course, we are talking 90 years later!

Christmas is just a couple days away and I bought Ray's Christmas present today. Got him a beautiful wristwatch. Is the only gift I am buying this year. The furniture Betts and I bought for the new apartment is our Christmas present to Mother and

Daddy.

EDITOR'S NOTE: Early 1930's! This had to be a very classy expensive Bulova watch to pay this much 90 years ago!

Christmas Day and just like spring! Ray gave me an exquisite evening purse, crocheted pearls over black, just what I needed. He was crazy about the watch I gave him. I've never seen him so pleased. I didn't expect anything from the family, but I got a couple bottles of lovely perfume. Ray was here with me all evening.

Betty is so tickled. Karl got here today and he gave her an engagement ring! It's the most exquisite thing I've ever seen. One large diamond in a square cut platinum setting with six small ones on each side of it. 13 diamonds in all.

Betty and Karl

New Year's Eve, 1933. Had a glorious New Year's Eve. Six of us went together to the McAlfin Hotel and had a glorious time. We left here at 4:30 and went back to Ray's house in Jersey, then over to the Saxons, who were going on an all night party. Betty and Karl are going to the opera tomorrow afternoon so they wanted to go home and get some rest.

This ends my 1933 diary. Tomorrow starts a new year!

1934

The New Year's Eve party last night at the Saxtons didn't break up until noon today so we all went to sleep over there. Got up about 3:00 and Ray and I went back to his house and we were so tired. We slept over there and didn't get up until 8:00 tonight.

Karl and Betty went to the Firestone broadcast tonight, but Ray and I couldn't make it. Got to my house about 10 PM and the boys stayed till 12 then started back for Jersey. It was a glorious New Year's celebration!

What a cold, what a cold! It's in my head and chest and all over me now. Didn't do much of anything all day today. Ray came over tonight and we decided to see a movie. Drove clear over to the Bronx in search of something we wanted to see. Finally ended up at the Colosseum and saw John Barrymore in "The Counselor at Law ". Pretty punk.

Nickie came over early this evening and we went up to the Colosseum to see "Son of Kong " a sequel to "King Kong". I was so disappointed in it, it was so awful it was funny. "King Kong" was so marvelous I thought this one would be too.

Didn't feel any too good today, so I just loafed around. I must have practiced too hard yesterday and pulled my insides to pieces. I hurt all over.

I hated to leave Nickie, but we had to go. The boat isn't bad and there's quite a nice crowd on board. Betts and I are dead tired so we're going to turn in early. We sailed at 6 PM tonight.

The boat got to Providence at six this morning and we changed to the bus for Boston. Staying at the LaSalle Hotel where we always stay when we're here. The Broadway Club is where we're going to be working. It's just a couple of blocks away. it's a lovely place. Used to be the Mayfair. We open tonight and although there was not a huge crowd, we got a very good hand. Only four acts, two shows a night, 7:30 and 11:30. Lou Walters, who booked us in and Harry Drake were there for the last show, and took us over for some coffee at the Bradford Roof.

Pretty stiff today but not nearly as bad as I expected after all our dancing last night. Took a long walk this afternoon and it was such a nice day. Had some trouble with our music the first show but everything else was fine for the second show. Hope it stays that way. Quite a good crowd and we got good hands. It is truly a lovely club. April 11, 1934.

Had such a good shows tonight. During the last show, we finished our high kick number right on the dot of 12, and the orchestra broke into happy birthday. The MC, Lou Ash, made a nice speech about us and it being our birthday tonight and all of us had a lot of fun. Harry took us to eat after the second show. I came home to the hotel between shows and it's a good thing I did because Nickie phoned me . I was so surprised and happy! April 20, 1934 and at the stroke of midnight, it was April 21!

Today is our birthday! Had such a lovely birthday today. Had lots of wires and cards. Mother sent us eight pairs of stockings and daddy had our car all fixed up for us. I didn't get Ray's gift yet. He's mailing it today, he thought I'd be home in time. Lou Walters gave us a big box of candy. Eddie Louis gave us each a lovely corsage of gardenias and tiny rose buds, and they had a big party in our honor after the shows. We surely had a grand birthday! We are 24 today. Ray called me from New York again tonight. Love him so!

Started our third week in Boston, hope we can go home next Sunday. I'm getting homesick. Shopped all afternoon for a hat, but couldn't find one. Betts and I went to the Met with Don Stiles between shows, saw "Bottoms Up "and it's a good stage show with George Raft. After the second show, we went out with Lou Walters and Harry and had fried chicken.

Nickie's birthday gift to me came tonight. It's a lovely folding camera. Something I've always wanted. I am so tickled with it!

Had a good time tonight after the last show. We had to do four shows tonight and we were so tired we could hardly move, but we went over to the Mayfair with Lou Walters and Harry and Al and then to the Congress Inn. We surely have been going out a lot these three weeks. Lou and Harry have been grand to us.

Poured rain all day today. Had a letter from Nicki that made me really homesick for him. He called me up from New York tonight at 9:15. Had another wire from Lou Weiss and it's all set for us to open in Detroit next Thursday at $175. Not a very good salary but the idea is for us to keep working. We're leaving for New York

Sunday morning and will have to leave for Detroit Monday. I'll hardly get to see Nicki at all.

Our bus left at 9 o'clock this morning and got into New York at 6 PM. It was a beautiful day for the trip, but I was so tired after the first couple of hours. Nickie met me in New York, and I was so tickled to see him. He looks great. Betty expected Jack to be there, but he didn't show up, nor did he call all evening. Mother and Daddy are fine and it's great to be home again. We decided not to leave for Detroit until Tuesday morning. It will only take a day and a half to drive there and we don't open until Thursday night.

What a treat to sleep in my own soft Simmons mattress last night after sleeping in a hard hotel bed for three weeks. Had such a shock today. We stopped in to see Jack's mother and she said that Jack got married Saturday to Emmy Clark. They hardly knew each other. She roped him in good and plenty. He can't even support himself, let alone a wife. Had dinner downtown with Nickie tonight. Won't see him again for a couple weeks.

EDITOR'S NOTE: So THAT is the reason why Jack did not meet Betty when they arrived in New York!

Left New York at 7:30 this morning, had a grand day for the trip and the car just flew along. Got in Cleveland about 10 PM, 530 miles. We are all dead tired. The first day of the trip is always exhausting.

Didn't get away from Cleveland until 8:30 this morning but only had a short distance to go so we took it easy. Got in Detroit about 2 PM and had an awful time finding a place to stay. Everything is full. There must be a boom or something here. Finally found a lovely apartment on W. Grand Blvd., about eight blocks from the Oriole Terrace where we'll be working. The apartment is grand and Mother can cook for us so it will be cheaper than a hotel. Going to bed early, so tired.

The heat here is fierce. I guess summer is here to stay for good as this is the beginning of May. Drove Mother around to a few stores and the traffic here is enough to drive you crazy. Betty went out with a friend this afternoon, Jamie Edgar. He certainly is nice. The son of a big millionaire here and they own several huge estates. Too bad one person has to have so much money. One of his homes he showed Betts had 21 bedrooms. Had a sweet letter from Nickie today, picked it up over at the club. Good crowds at the club tonight

Had to do a matinee show at 2:00 PM today. It seems so silly. It's the first time I've ever done a show in the middle of the afternoon in a nightclub. It was for a luncheon crowd. Jamie was supposed to meet us and take us for a boat ride and he was coming to the club tonight and take us out after the shows, but he didn't show up at all. That's the trouble with these rich fellows, they're so spoiled. No matter what they do, they think it's right. The club was packed tonight. Wonderful audience with huge applause! No letter from my Nickie today.

I had fun taking some photos with my new camera yesterday, but got the pictures we took, and they're awful. The sun was too bright and we were frowning and had the sun grins and everything else. Next time, we will know better. I love this new camera and it is going to be grand once I understand the do's s and don'ts of it.

We landed another job today. We open at the Fox Theater here next Friday for one week. As long as we're going to be here that long, I guess we'll start making the very best of it. Then we will drive down to Indianapolis for a few days.

I am so disgusted and disappointed. I hardly care what happens now. We went to the Fox this morning and ran through our dances so they could build two big production numbers around us, and after we got home, we found a message from Mr. Eisele, the manager, who had gone to New York, saying he couldn't use us after all, because another act had been booked at the Fox theater that he didn't know about. So now we can't stay over and we won't be able to collect our money and I won't even see Freddie. It's awful.

Another hot sweltering day. Drove Mother downtown and nearly perished with the heat. Ordered 50 photos from Maurice and got them today. Didn't have any left from the other batch.

There was a terrible fire in Chicago today, the worst fire since the one in 1871, which destroyed the whole city. This one was down in the southside and destroyed a whole square mile, an area of 120 acres. All the stockyard area was burned, thousands of cattle. It started at 4 PM and wasn't under control until 10 PM.

EDITOR'S NOTE: There had been less than 4 inches of rain since the beginning of the year and this fire occurred on May 19, 1934, and temperatures were hitting 92° on the day the fire started. A carelessly tossed cigarette in the stockyard caused the worst fire in Chicago since 1871. Six square blocks were destroyed. 1600 firefighters worked hard to extinguish this horrible fire.

Six square blocks of Chicago was destroyed by this fire.

If the heat doesn't break soon, everyone will fall over and die. I've never known it to be so hot. It was the hottest day yet but about 6 PM the heat broke and the rain came down in torrents. It even hailed. Today was the first time it had rained in 42 days, and the whole country was dried up. Crops all ruined and cattle starving. So this rain was surely welcome. I hope it keeps up for a couple of days.

I had the grandest surprise today. Freddie called me up and I had no idea he was in Chicago. He came into town yesterday, and I didn't even know it, and just sat around reading a book all day. He's busy today, but he'll be back early tomorrow so I will get to see him. I am so tickled. Had two letters from Ray today. He read about the fire here and was so worried.

Freddie Daw

Betts and I decided to drive to Indianapolis over the weekend to see Grandfather because we don't know when we will be able to see him if we don't work in Chicago this summer. So we started at 10 o'clock this morning and got in Indianapolis at two. There's room here at the house for us so we'll stay here.

Left Indianapolis at 7 o'clock this morning and got in Chicago at 11 AM, made 200 miles in four hours. Not bad. Mother is fine, but she was so lonesome over the weekend without us. Freddie got back from Detroit today so I saw him. He took me to supper at the Blackhawk hotel. They have a grand orchestra there, Seymour Simmons, and a good floor show. Had a dandy time. Didn't get in until 2:30 AM.

Saw Freddie tonight and had such a good time. Went to 222 North Clark St. to hear Cleo, a marvelous pianist, then to Able's for some beer, then back to 222, and it was closing so we went to another little club, where we had a few beers and then home.

Such a hot blistering day, just sat around and read all day and tried to keep cool. Met Freddie downtown at seven and I had another nice time with him tonight. I always enjoy myself so much when I am out with him. He's going on the road again tomorrow and will be out for about three weeks, so I guess it will be a long time before I will see him again because I think we're going back to New York next week. No job in sight yet and our money is just about gone.

This is the hottest weather in history for this time of the year. It is the first day of June. The official temperature was 102° today. People dropped off like flies. We all had to go to a movie that was air cooled to cool off. Saw a splendid picture, Dick Powell in

"20,000 Sweethearts". He is surely good and it is so grand that we are good friends.

It was such a long boring day today. All I did was take a walk and read a book. All our money is gone and we haven't landed a job, so we will have to go back to New York next week. I am so discouraged.

Gave an audition this afternoon for the Drake Hotel. They liked us very much and even discussed salary. We have to go back and see Mr. Duke Yalman and see whether or not we get the job. I surely hope so. It won't be for two weeks yet, and we could go to New York in the meanwhile and pick up some summer clothes.

Well, we signed the contract today for the Silver Forest Room at the Drake Hotel. I'm so tickled. We open the 18th so we're going to New York tomorrow and stay a few days then come back. We're going to leave about 8:00 in the morning and it shouldn't take us more than two days. I'm so excited about going home, and then coming back for this great job.

## SILVER FOREST
### DINER MODERNE
*Served from 6 p.m. to 9:30 p.m.*
*$2.50 per person*

❁ ❁

*Choice*

| | |
|---|---|
| Fruit Supreme Parisienne | Stuffed Deviled Egg |
| Chilled Pineapple or Tomato Juice | |
| Cold Jellied Consomme | Fresh Crabmeat Cocktail |
| Cream of Shrimps aux Croutons | Consomme des Viveurs |

❁

| | |
|---|---|
| Mixed Olives | Celery Hearts |
| Melba Toast | Saltine Crackers |

❁

*Choice*

Grilled Jumbo Whitefish Maitre d'Hotel Butter
Vol au Vent of Fresh Seafood Dahlberg
Loin Lamb Chop Saute with Mushrooms
Roast Milk Fed Chicken, Corn Dressing, Stewed Prunes
Galantine of Capon and Prague Ham, Melon Balls in Jelly

**Our Chef Recommends**
Mignon of Beef Tenderloin Bordelaise, Braised Celery 2.75
Baked Filet of English Sole in Lobster Shell Blackstone 2.75
Grilled Selected Sirloin Steak Maitre d'Hotel Butter 3.25

❁

| | |
|---|---|
| Cauliflower au Gratin | Potato Anna |
| Buttered String Beans | Candied Sweet Potatoes |

❁

Hearts of Lettuce Lorenzo Dressing

❁

| | |
|---|---|
| Cheese and Crackers | Individual Apple Pie |
| Homemade Cake | Stewed Peaches |
| Sunshine Cake a la Mode | |
| Choice of Ice Cream or Sherbet | Strawberry Sundae |

❁

**Coffee   Tea   Milk**

a Dessert worthy of your consideration
**Drake Frozen Pudding Rum Sauce   35 cents**

❁ ❁

1934 Menu from Silver Forest ballroom

Ballroom (stage in background with Christmas trees)

We left New York and got into Chicago about 4:30 this afternoon and it was surely a rotten trip. The roads are all torn up all the way through and we had a flat tire which two truck drivers changed for us. Finally got in and didn't do much except get all unpacked and settled. Have a nice big apartment and really like it. Had a sweet letter from Ray this morning.

Had a nice time today. Drove down to the Drake to step off our routines on the floor, then drove out to the Villa to see good friends.

EDITOR'S NOTE: the Drake Hotel was built in 1920. Visiting royalty, heads of state, and even well-known gangsters stayed there.

EDITOR'S NOTE: Theo Rooms was the head chef at the Drake Hotel, and he is the person who invented thousand island dressing!

Went to rehearsal at three and went over all of our music with the band. It's a very good band here at the Drake, but there's no violins, and we really need them in our dances. Opened tonight and we did three shows, 8:30 PM and 10 PM and 12 midnight. We went over just fine.

The William Morris office called and wanted us to open at the Blossom in Detroit, but we told them we were under contract and working. They wanted us to take some photos down to them, so we did and while I was downtown, I looked around for a gift for Freddie's birthday, but couldn't find anything.

We just stayed in all day and read because it was quite cool out. Discovered that the front bumper of our car had been stolen. Just taken clear off. How can people be so low? Thank goodness our insurance will take care of it. Had pretty good shows tonight, quite a grand crowd.

Had such a good time today. Didn't have to work, no Sunday shows, so I spent the whole day with Freddie. He came for me about 2:00, and we took a long drive out in the country, then back downtown to the Blackhawk, where the band had to play from 8:00 to 9:30 PM. It sounded so good. I had supper there while Freddie played in his orchestra. Then we went out to the Harlem Nut House and had some beer and saw a show. Got home at 4:00 AM.

Betts and I drove downtown today and bought a record and an orchestration of "Mood Indigo". We're going to put in a new dance on Monday and we decided to get something easy to fit "Mood Indigo". So we borrowed a Victrola and practiced all afternoon. Made up a really cute dance.

Another sweltering day. Had to stay in the house to keep cool. Mother made Betts a lovely white organdy dress, semi formal. She went out tonight with Earl and wanted something new to wear. I seem to be the family chauffeur lately. Heard from Nickie and he got the job that he was after. He seems all enthusiastic about it so I hope it turns out to be something good.

No, the heat hasn't broken yet so Betts and I went to a movie to keep cool. Saw little Shirley Temple in "Little Miss Marker". She certainly is a marvel. Came home and slept all evening. No shows tonight so nothing to do.

Shirley Temple

Much cooler today even though it is late July. The awful heat finally broke. Started to make a new dress, white organdy with eyelet embroidery. It's going to be a sem- formal dress, very long with a ruffle around the bottom, and very low in the back. Sewed on it all day. Have no machine though so I have to do it all by hand.

Freddie got in from Louisville about four this afternoon and he took me out tonight. Went to the Campton Tea Gardens, another club and ended up at the Triangle for waffles. Had such a good time. It's been a long time since I've been out. He looks fine, lost 5 pounds.

We intend to leave for New York Thursday so I got a few last-minute things attended to. Had the radio in the car fixed and it cost me $4.50. Bought a jack for the car, we lost the one we had. Had another good time tonight. Freddie came for me about six and we celebrated with a last good time in Chicago. Has supper at the great restaurant that I love downtown, then went to the State on the lake and saw a peachy show, then to the Crystal bar, then the 100 Club, then the High Hat Club. Got home at 4:30 am.

Went swimming with Freddie today July 1, 1934. Didn't go till late so I didn't get sunburn. Went to a beach way up north in no man's land. Had a dandy time. We came back here to dress, then he took me out to supper. Got home early about 12:30.

Got up at five this morning so we could get into New York by noon, but we discovered we had a flat tire when we got out the car, the same one we had trouble with yesterday. So we had to unpack the whole trunk loaded with clothes and costumes, to get the spare off, then we had to stay in the next town to get the bum tire fixed in case we had another flat. From Sacramento to New York we ran into heavy Sunday traffic and just crawled along. Didn't get home until 5 PM. 5 AM to 5 PM, 12 long hours!

Del Mar Beach, New Jersey 1930's

I'm going down to the shore with Ray over the weekend. His family has a cottage at Del Mar Beach, so we're going down Friday evening and staying through Sunday. So I had to go downtown today and buy some shoes to go with my new white organdy dress. Met Ray over in Jersey tonight, had supper with him and then we all went to the Sexton's and had such a good time.

Just poured and poured all day. Had a regular flood here. The ocean was almost up to the boardwalk. Couldn't do much of anything but sit in the house and talk and eat candy. Took a ride in the rain in Ed's open car and got soaked. Ray and I aren't going to drive home until tomorrow morning. We're afraid to go tonight in the rain; the traffic will be so heavy and probably a few accidents.

Nickie and I left Del Mar this morning about 7:30 and got to Jersey City about 9:30. Ray had to go on to work so I came on home on the subway. I was dead tired so I went to bed about noon and slept till 4:30. There was a letter here for me from Freddie.

Had a long hard day today. Rehearsed from noon until six, then again from 8 to 10. Ray called for me and we went up to Bob Houser's place on 92nd St. and Broadway. So tired I could not enjoy myself.

The costumers came today and took orders for the costumes. Had to rehearse late again tonight. We start at noon every day and end at either six, or sometimes we have to go back after supper and rehearse until after 10 o'clock. The show is shaping up fine. I think it's going to be a peach. Saw the sketches for our costumes and they're simply beautiful.

Got through rehearsals at six tonight but it took us over an hour to drive home. I never saw it raining so hard in my life. It was a regular flood. Ray and Ed had a date to come over here at 8:30 and they didn't show up until 10:30. Ray's car was flooded twice and he had to stop and wait for it to get dried out. Rainy September!

Oh, more rehearsals today, didn't have to go until 2 PM and we got through at 5:30. I asked Ray to take me over to Elizabeth, New Jersey tonight. I wanted to see another unit and the show that they put on at the Ritz theater. Their show is called "Words and Music". It was surely good. We open at the Ritz on Saturday.

More rehearsals from 2 to 6 today. We certainly have had easy rehearsals on this job. Tomorrow we don't have to go until 7 PM, but we have to be at the costumers at 2:00 for fittings.

Our last day of rehearsals. We open tomorrow at the Ritz theater. Ray drove us over tonight about 10 and we checked in the hotel. We have to be at the theater tomorrow at 8 AM, so everyone came over tonight.

Stage of the Ritz Theater

Had to be at the theater for rehearsal at 8 o'clock this morning. Only three shows every day. By the time we did the third show tonight, everything was shaping up fine. I think the unit is going to be great. It needs a few changes; the lights and music are still not perfect yet. But everyone is crazy about it and for an opening day, it was a huge success.

Had marvelous shows today and packed houses. Ray came over last night and tonight too. Mother and Daddy are coming tomorrow to see the shows.

Closed at the Ritz tonight. The last show was absolutely grand. Everyone went over so well. After the final show, we all celebrated, because the audiences have been so grand at every performance. I must admit, that Betts and I really seemed to steal the show every night! Ray came again and drove us home. Layoff tomorrow and Thursday. We open in Philadelphia on Friday.

Betts and I went downtown today and bought hats and shoes and spent the rest of the day packing our trunk. Have to leave tomorrow. Ray came over tonight. He's going to try to get over to Philadelphia Sunday to see me.

We are in Philadelphia now. We have a dandy big room at the hotel and we open tomorrow at the Fox theater. Betty and I went there tonight to see the show and it was surely punk.

EDITOR'S NOTE: the Fox Theater opened in 1923 and features 2,423 seats. The stage is 60 feet wide. The Jazz Singer, the first "talkie" motion picture, was shown here.

We opened at Fox today and what a terrible theater. I'll be glad when we get this booking over with, and start playing at the really fine theaters. Only three shows a day here and none on Sunday. The first two shows today were awful but everything was fine on the third one and we were very pleased with the crowd's reaction.

Had four shows today and I am dead tired tonight. Dottie and Betts went to a party but I expect Ray tomorrow so I don't want to go out and drink and feel punk. Had good shows today.

Had such a lovely day. No shows at all, so Ray drove in from New Jersey and spent the day with me. He's not going back until tomorrow morning because he has to stop on the way on business and he can make it all in one trip.

Our friend Suzanne came to see us today. She lives here in town, and it was wonderful seeing her. She came back to the theater with us and watched the show from backstage. She really seem fascinated by it all.

Mother and Daddy drove in from New York to see us today. They saw the supper show and visited with us for a while and then they left before the last show. Had a sweet letter from Nickie today.

Closed at the Fox today. Leave tomorrow morning on the bus for Wilmington, Delaware.

In Wilmington, Delaware now. Got in at nine and went right to the theater for rehearsal. It's a very tiny theater; it's almost impossible to work on that stage. Four shows a day and they really don't need more than two. We're all disgusted. We couldn't even hang the scenery.

The shows weren't so bad today. Every performance was packed. The last one was just peachy. No shows at all tomorrow so we're going to New York for the day. I would go crazy in this awful town with nothing to do.

Had a glorious time today. We left Wilmington last night after the last show and caught the 11:30 train to New York. Got in at 1:40 AM and took the subway home. Mother and Daddy were so tickled to see us. We wired them we were coming.

EDITOR'S COMMENT; It is amazing to me that two beautiful young ladies are totally comfortable taking trains and subways very late at night into the morning hours and feel perfectly safe.

Ray came over to the house about 4:00 and had supper with us and then he and I went out. It was so grand seeing him again even though it's been only a week.

Another long dreary day. Four shows in this town seems so unnecessary. Only the last one is good. Had a sweet letter from Nickie. I hear from him every day. His letters are the best part of each day to me. I'll see him again next week. We lay off Sunday, Monday and Tuesday.

So warm again today and yesterday it was freezing. I'm catching another cold. Guess I'll have to get to work on the cod liver oil. Benny came to work today with an upset stomach and felt so punk they had to send out for a bed for him. He took all the shows easy. Mother sent us a box today with some new dancing shoes and some cookies she baked, thank goodness.

Hershey Theater, 1900 seats, built in 1933. Continues to be a premier performing arts center.

Opened in Hershey, Pennsylvania today at the Hershey theater. Such a gorgeous place. We're only here for two days, today and tomorrow. Only had to do one show today at 8:45 PM. Have to do three tomorrow. Have a three day layoff after this date so we are going to New York.

Had three shows today, the first two were not too crowded but the last one was great and really packed. We're all taking the bus to New York tonight. Have Sunday, Monday and Tuesday off. This Hershey date was grand. I'm sorry that it wasn't longer.

The trip on the bus last night was just awful. Didn't get home until 7 AM this morning and we were dead tired. Went right to bed and slept till 3 o'clock. Nickie came over at 5:00 and I was so tickled to see him. He had dinner with us, and then he and I went out for a drive.

Went downtown today and stopped in the business office to see about the bus tomorrow night. We open an Allentown, Pennsylvania, on Wednesday, and we all have to take the bus tomorrow night. Saw Ray again tonight and had such a grand time with him.

EDITOR'S NOTE: The Colonial Theater was built in 1920 and was known as the "Glamour Cinema of the central business district."

We opened up the Colonial Theater in Allentown today. It's quite a lovely theater and the orchestra isn't bad. We will be doing three shows a day here.

1930's street car

We rode in from Allentown to Easton on the street car this morning. Took over an hour and it was so freezing cold. We opened at the State Theater with four shows a day. I wanted to go home to New York, but it was too far for just one day.

The new act went in the last show tonight. They certainly are hokey, but that's what the bookers wanted. They dress as sailors and spit water all over the stage and do a lot of fast tumbling. Personally, I don't like them, but if it helps the show, that's what counts.

Back in New York and slept late and caught up on some lost sleep. It feels so good to sleep in my own bed. Met Ray about 53:0 and had supper at his house and then we went out. We had a grand time. I'll see him when I'm playing in Brooklyn too.

Betts and I each bought a new coat today. I got a lovely brown one trimmed in fur with a muff to match. So pretty. Paid $60 for it and I got a bargain. Bought shoes and a hat too. Saw Ray again tonight.

Madison Theater, Brooklyn, N. Y.

EDITOR'S NOTE: The Madison Theater opened in 1914 and housed 450 people in the orchestra and 150 more in the balcony.

Opened at the Madison Theater in Brooklyn today and what a grand theater it is. The orchestra is just peachy. The show looks so good, it is a big musical production. We have four shows a day here. We played to standing room only all day today. Ray came over and saw the last show and really loved it. He drove us home later that night.

Had today off. Ray and I went to a party at the Sexton's and had a good time but the liquor wasn't very good and I feel lousy.

Train in the 1930's

Left on the train this morning for Pittsburgh. It was a 12 1/2 hour trip and I was so sick all the way. That liquor last night got me. I really don't drink much at all but I felt terrible. I hope it didn't make Ray sick too. Got in Pittsburgh at 10 PM. Staying at the Roosevelt Hotel.

We opened at the Pitt Theater today. It's not a very grand place, very small and a rotten orchestra, but from now on, we play the big houses only. The show is all set now. It's going over very well here though; we were surprised. The audiences seem to really love us. We're going to be here a week.

Had five shows today and I am dead on my feet. No shows tomorrow so I am going to rest and rest and rest. Had a sweet letter from Nickie. He said he was terribly sick from that liquor at the Saxon's party too. I guess it was kind of bad.

It was so great as I was just loafing around today. Slept till 1:00, then went out and ate and bought the Sunday papers. Betts and I had our pictures in the paper today, a big three column one, the double head, so nice. We had a special delivery letter from Mother today. She is sending us our pink costumes that she made.

EDITOR' NOTE: big 3 column photo in Sunday paper.

So disappointed today. Heard some bad news. We were to play the Earl theater in Washington next week and then we were supposed to go back to the Colosseum in New York and I was so tickled because it meant seeing Ray and the family again. But instead of going to New York, we go to the Palace in Cleveland. It's a much better date, but it means we won't get back to New York for six weeks. Ray will have a fit when he gets my letter about it.

Closed tonight in Pittsburgh. It was a long terrible week. One of the line girls bumped into a trunk backstage in the dark and cracked one of her front teeth out and chipped two others. Such a rotten shame. Poor kid.

Got in Washington at 9 o'clock this morning. Staying at the Annapolis Hotel and playing the Earl theater. A lovely house and such a marvelous orchestra. The audience is a bit tough but Betts and I went over great all day today.

Jimmy Savo.....1893 to 1960, pantomimist.

Jimmy Savo is in the show with us this week as an extra added attraction. He's marvelous, gets $2500 a week, a hokey comedian known as the worlds greatest Pantomimist. They call him the "midget strongman", but he is not a midget, but just a short little guy who wears big baggy clothes. I love Washington. It's going to be a pleasant week.

Annapolis Theater

We only had three shows today, and they were all so good. I really do enjoy working here so much. Betts and I get grand hands. Jessie Brown, and her husband, who is the major general of the US Army, very good friends of Mother, took us driving today, and they came to see the first show. Such lovely people.

Jessie Brown came to see the show again. She brought along a friend and they came back to our dressing room afterward. A commercial photographer took a lot of photos of me to use in telephone ads. I wish I could see them.

We opened at the Palace Theater in Cleveland today. Our first show was supposed to be at 12:30 and our train didn't even get in until 12:15. It was certainly a mad rush getting ready but we finally got on at 1:30. They really liked the show here and it goes over fine. We are staying at the Carter Hotel.

Had such wonderful shows today. Betts and I get a tremendous hand every performance! The show looks great here at the Palace.

I woke up this morning and it was snowing hard. This certainly is a change from the weather in Washington last week. Mother sent us some new dancing shoes and they came tonight special delivery. Had really grand shows today.

What a blue Monday this has been. We had to go to a luncheon at the Variety Club at 11:30 this morning and put on a show for them. It certainly was a mess. Everything went wrong all day. Hopefully, the audience thought it was wonderful.

EDITOR'S NOTE: The Shea Theater in Toronto was built in 1914 and was the largest movie palace in Canada and the largest vaudeville theater in the world. It contains 12 opera boxes and a full size orchestra pit.

Opened at the Shea Theatre in Toronto, Canada today. Only three shows a day and none on Sunday. The audience is simply marvelous. Ours is the only stage show in town, and the people seem starved for it. They certainly are appreciative. Staying at the Ford hotel.

Had to do four shows today, being Saturday, and that huge theater was jammed for every single show. I thought it would be awfully cold up here in Canada but it's really very warm. Feels like spring. Didn't have a letter from Nickie today and now I have to wait till Monday. He is so wonderful about writing me every day when we are not together.

No shows today as it is Sunday. We had planned to go to Niagara Falls with Benny and Maxine but it takes four hours each way, so we gave it up. We rented a car and chauffeur, and drove around the city for an hour. Then we played cards all afternoon, seven of us, and ended up at a midnight show.

Betts and I bought the cutest little Persian cat today. It's a pedigree and only seven weeks old. Maxine bought one too and they're so cute together. Mother will probably have a fit when we take it home, but it will never be a nuisance like our other cat at home. He's so pretty, gray with little white markings on his face.

Had so much fun with the kittens in the theater today. We got their pedigree papers and Maxine's is two days older than ours. Hers is a blue Persian and ours is a gray Persian. They were both sired by the same male but they have different mothers. We named ours Dusty and Maxine calls her Smoky. We all just sit by the hour and watch them play. So cute. Had dandy shows all day today. Successful day all around.

Took Smoky and Dusty to be altered today, but they're too young. Have to wait until they are about 3 1/2 months old, and they are only 7 weeks now. They were at the vets all day and we missed them so. Nice letters from Nickie. We heard today that we lay off after Montreal. That is two weeks from now, so will get to go home sooner than we expected and I am so glad.

Four more shows today but I'd rather work on Sunday then be docked a day's salary. Nothing new today, no mail or anything. Played cards again tonight and won back $2.50 of what I lost last night.

Left Montreal at 10 o'clock this morning and got into New York at 8 PM. Had such a long tiresome trip on the train. Ray met us and drove us home. So tickled to see him. Mother and Daddy are fine and the apartment looks so sweet, all changed around. Mother was certainly surprised when we gave her the kitten. Our big cat is scared to death of it.

Mother and I went downtown to Clines today and try to get a dress for me but I've gotten so thin. I wanted to get a good silk dress, but all I managed to get was a little green woolen one. Guess I'll have to get a little more meat on me before I can get anything. Daddy, Ray and I went over to Elizabeth, New Jersey tonight to see a new show, entitled "Live Laugh and Love". I thought it was awful.

Met Ray in Jersey this evening and had dinner at his house. Took his mother a big box of candy. Nickie and I went out and had a grand time. Have to go away again tomorrow. This week's layoff has been grand. I feel so rested, and I've gained 3 pounds. Everybody had a fit because I had gotten so thin.

Left for Providence, Rhode Island on the boat this evening at 6 PM. It seems good to see all the company again. This is an awful old boat, so cold and uncomfortable. We get in early in the morning about 7 o'clock.

Opened at Fays Theater in Providence today and what a fun place. They've got a grand big picture of Betts and myself out front, a huge drawing of our double headshot.I'm going to try and get it when we close here. There's certainly is a punk audience here.

Had to do four shows today, only three every day after this. John Hickey is here from New York to see how the show is. They're working on a percentage here, and if business isn't really good, we will all have to take a small cut. Business was punk today, but I hope it picks up tomorrow. We went out this evening with some of the group and had some high balls. Good time.

Three shows today and business was grand and the audience was really enthusiastic. Certainly is cold here.

Open at the Albee in Brooklyn today. Such a nice theatre. I hope it will be a wonderful week. So good to be home again. Saw my Ray.

Closed tonight after two weeks. It surely was a nice time and the audience was grand. We open at the Palace tomorrow. It is quite an event to play at the Palace. It is the best there is.

EDITOR'S NOTE: The Palace Theatre faces Times Square and was built in 1913. It contains 1743 seats in a three level auditorium and also has boxes on the side walls.

Opened at the New York Palace today. It is such an old theater, but has a beautiful reputation, but the dressing rooms are awful. But you really have to be good to get to play here so I guess we're very lucky.

Betts and I are going over great at the Palace... Better than anyone else in the show for sure. This theatre has the reputation for excellent fine shows, and the audience is always enthusiastic and grand.

Today is Christmas Day, and we had to do four shows. It seems a shame to have to work on Christmas. Had fun in the theater though. Got some lovely personal stationary from Benny and Maxine, flowers from Nik, an atomizer from Jack, flowers from our backup girls. Mother and Daddy gave us underwear, bath robes, pajamas, etc. My Nickie gave me a stunning gold and jade bracelet. I've always wanted one.

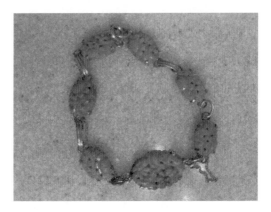

EDITOR'S NOTE: Jade bracelet; I have it now. There is an exquisite jade necklace also that I have, but perhaps it is given at a later date, because it has not been mentioned yet.

Closed at the Palace tonight and we had to get a bus right after the show for Troy, New York. Will be up there for New Year's and I'll miss going out with my Ray. Darn it. I had planned to have so much fun with him on New Year's Eve.

Opened at Proctors in Troy today. Only here for four days, then we lay off three days and go to Portland, Maine. Staying at the Hendrick Hudson hotel. This is a terrible town.

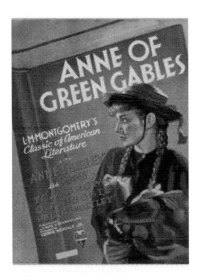

Our big production show is playing with a grand picture here, "Anne of Green Gables". I saw it today and it's so good. I have a terrible cold and feel rotten. I ache all over. Hope I don't get the grippe.

New Year's Eve and it was awful, not being home for it was just so sad for me. We closed here tonight, but had to do a midnight show. Such a mess. I am so missing Ray and the family. We all went out for a while afterward to the tavern. Had a pretty good time but I was so homesick. Have to stay here tomorrow and on Wednesday we go to Portland and open there on Friday. This is the end of the year and the end of my diary for 1934..

EDITOR'S NOTE: I am so extremely disappointed that the diary for the year 1935 is missing. The year 1935 is the year that Elizabeth, (Betty), broke her back while taking a curtain call on stage. She ended up in the hospital for many months. The doctors took a piece of her shin bone and with tiny gold wire, wrapped it against the break in her back. (Remember, this was 1937! ) She was in the hospital a long time and was quite frail for the rest of her life. The doctors also told her to never have children because her back would never stand the weight of pregnancy. Sadly, this terrible accident ended the Wheeler Twins career. I wish I had a day-to-day account of all of this. It is all hearsay from my mother, who told us the story many times. However, I found several photos in the press book that I made for my mom that were taken during the year 1935. These are the photos that I found...

Theatrical Night

in the **Bacchante**

TONIGHT

Featuring stars of the Parisienne Scandals, now appearing at Fay's Theatre, in an impromptu bit of sparkling entertainment. Jack Pepper . . . Terry Howard . . . Wheeler Twins . . . Mlle. Ayres and M. Rene and dancers from the Moulin Rouge.

No Cover Charge—BILLY LOSSEZ MUSIC

3-31-35    Rhode Island

Providence BILTMORE

*Wheeler Twins Routine Liked by Everybody*

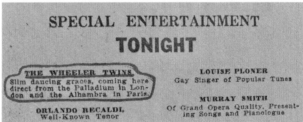

EDITOR'S NOTE: I will now begin my mother's diary for 1936...

January 1, 1936.

Had a grand time at the party last night. A real New Year's Eve celebration. It didn't break up until 6 AM this morning. Ray and I went back to his house and slept until 2 PM. We both feel a little bit shaky and rocky today! I guess everyone who was out that night feels the same way today. Got home to my house at 5:30 PM and Mother and Daddy and Betts were just getting up ....too much fun on New Year's Eve!

It was pouring rain today, and the ice was melting and it was so slippery. Ray could hardly drive. I was so nervous for him. A heavy fog too.

Hal and Ray came up for supper tonight. I made a big chocolate layer cake and it was grand. Ray brought a quart of port and sherry and we celebrated the raise he got today. He's leaving on a trip Monday. He's making out so well in his job and they gave him another line to handle and he's on a 10% commission now instead of 3%. Things are beginning to break now, thank goodness!

EDITOR'S NOTE: This MGM movie came out at the beginning of 1935 with a budget of $1,950,000. The box office brought in $4,460,000. Huge success!

Mother and I saw a wonderful movie tonight. Charles Laughton in "Mutiny on the Bounty". I think it is the best picture I have ever seen.

Hard rain all day so I didn't go out. My linens came from Macy's so I put them all away. I have so many nice things now. Ray may get home tomorrow night. I hope so. I miss him so very much.

Had such an exciting afternoon. Mother and I went down to Macy's white sale and I bought a a lot of things for my trousseau. Bed linen, table linen, bathroom stuff. Spent $60. If I don't buy while I have the money, I will never get it. My darling Nickie called me tonight. He's in New Haven now. He'll be home Saturday and leave again Sunday. Our time together seems so short. I miss him so much when we are not together.

Went downtown today and bought Ray a lovely wine red silk dressing robe. He needs one so badly, so I got it for him now instead of his birthday in March and he can be using it while he travels. I wanted to take advantage of the sales now too. It was a $20 robe and I only paid $14.80 for it. Ray left for Boston today for a three day convention. He'll be traveling pretty steadily from now on so I guess I just better get used to it and make the best of it. But I do miss him so much.

January, 1936.

Had such a nice time tonight. Ray and Hal took Betts and me to the hockey game at Madison Square Garden. The game was rather slow. Boston and Americans 2 to 1, but it's the first game I ever saw and I enjoyed it so much. Starting to snow again tonight and the last snowstorm is still frozen solid and has left inches of ice all over the city.

It got warmer this morning, and the snow melted a little, then it immediately froze over and the ice covers everything. I never saw such a streak of below zero weather. There's a shortage of coal and milk and people are suffering. Worst of all through the middle west.

Ray left on another trip today. This is awful; he's going away so much. I was almost tempted to go with him this time. If this new arrangement of his job works out all right we'll get married soon and then I'll be perfectly happy. I love him so.

Valentine's Day, 1936. Ray sent me a grand big Valentine box of candy from Springfield and he phoned me tonight. It made me so homesick for him. He's only been gone since Tuesday but it seems like weeks. Bill Blaine and Connie Beard invited themselves over tonight. I actually get sick when I look at Bill now that he's home, I hope he doesn't get in the habit of coming up here often. He'll get a very cold reception from me if he does.

It turned so warm today and the snow and ice melted so fast. The thaw caused so much damage because of the ice. Betts and I took a walk, but we almost needed hip boots. Had another sweet letter from Ray. I hear from him every day. I started to knit a sweater, and it's going to be so pretty, a soft shade of blue.

I went out for a walk today. Hadn't been out for a few days because of the frigid weather. I only go out if I really need to. Thought I'd go to a movie, but I didn't have enough money. This rotten weather, I wish it would go away.

I sent Grandfather five dollars for his birthday a couple of days ago. And I finished the belt of my sweater, now I'm stuck till I can get some more wool for the sleeves. It surely is pretty. Betty is making one too, but she's crocheting hers instead of knitting it.

Our cat Ginger is going to have kittens. Our other cat, the big Persian, is the father. They put one over on us, that is for sure. I guess she'll have the kittens in two or three weeks. My goodness, two cats are bad enough, without four or five more.

We all spent the afternoon and evening playing a new game, it is called "Monopoly". It has taken the country by storm.

We had such a lovely time together, but Ray had to go back to Boston again tonight, so I saw him off on the midnight train. I hated to see him go, but he'll be back in about a week.

Surprise today.......

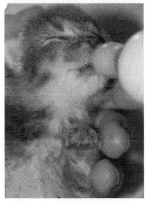

What a day, my goodness! Ginger had her kittens this afternoon, and none of us can do anything but sit and watch them. She only had two, a brown and red one like herself, and a pearl gray one like Tuffy, and they both have Tuffy's long Persian hair. So very cute. The new kittens are two days old now and so cute. They seem about three times larger than when they were born. They are so fat and full of milk. They can hardly move. They don't open their eyes for nine days. Rhoda came up tonight and we all played Monopoly all evening.

I felt so blue all day long. Didn't have a letter from Ray and Betty was so excited about getting dolled up in a new evening dress and going out with Hal tonight, and I had nothing to do. But at 7 o'clock Ray phoned me from Rochester, and then, of course, I felt better. I thought he might be home this weekend, but he said he can't make it until next weekend. Heck.

A beautiful spring day for March so I took a walk and went to a movie. Saw Ginger Rogers and Fred Astaire in "Follow the Fleet". It was surely good.

So many people think I look like Ginger Rogers. It's just my hair I guess. Had a letter and card from Ray today. He is in Buffalo now.

EDITOR'S NOTE: Ginger Rogers above and Elinor below... Many people think they favored each other.

Had such a grand time tonight. Ray and Hal took Betts and me to the circus. I hadn't been since I was little and I enjoyed it so. But the best thing of all was what Ray brought me tonight, a photo of himself, beautifully framed. Such a splendid picture, so natural. I've wanted one ever since I've known him, five years, and at last I have one. It means more to me than anything I have.

Ray Nichols Age 29 years old

April 21, 1936. Another birthday rolled around and we are 26 years old today. I hope I am married before I have another birthday. Poor Betts is sick in bed with the grippe and this time last year she was in the hospital. Ray is out of town, but he sent me a very lovely leather purse and a pair of beige kid gloves. Everything I got I surely needed.

However, the very best gift I have gotten from Ray was a pair of 8" tall exquisite dancing porcelain figurines which represent "The Wheeler Twins".

EDITOR's NOTE: I have them proudly displayed in my living room, and have had them for many years. Priceless to me!

No letter from Ray today, hope I get a special from him tomorrow. Started to make a cute luncheon set this evening, cloth and four matching napkins.

I finished my luncheon set, all but the appliqué work. I am going to embroider little pots of cactus in the corners. Tomorrow I'm going to cut out a dress and start making it.

Another nice letter from Ray. I miss him so. I do hope he can get home this weekend.

We all went to a new movie tonight and saw a grand picture. "Showboat". I had a nice long letter from Ray. I have been so lonesome for him.

Tonight was the big fight (June 16, 1936) between Joe Louis and Max Schmeling. Everyone was certain that Louis would win early in the fight but Schmeling knocked him out in the 12th round. The odds were 8 to 1 against Schmeling, but he surprised everyone. The papers will surely be full of it tomorrow. Today is

June 19, 1936, a day that will go down in sports history.

Had a sweet letter from my Ray. I surely miss him. When he goes away I am so lonely for him. Betts took a sun bath on the roof; she's as black as can be. I've lost all my tan. When Ray was here over the weekend he ordered a rubber bathing suit for me. It won't come till next week. I can't wait to see it. I had a white one last year, but I wore it out. The one Ray is getting me is turquoise and is the new style with pleated trunks.

Had two letters from Ray and a card today. He sent me a check for five dollars to get a new bathing suit because I had to send the other one back. It was way too big for me. Took a long walk after supper.

Another hot July day, and another sun bath and another nice long letter from Ray. He won't be able to come home this weekend. He's staying in Boston till Monday and expects to be home the following Friday or Saturday. I'm so lonesome for him I don't know what to do. The time goes so slowly when he's away. The weekends are especially lonely.

I've heard from Ray every single day. Got a long letter from him today. Bless his sweet old heart.

Saw Louise off on the 4:30 train this afternoon for Chicago. She was here six weeks with us, and we only expected her to stay a few days, a week at the most. She surely did wear out her welcome. We were glad to see her go.

Didn't see Ray tonight, so I spent the evening cutting out a robe for myself. It's going to be so pretty. The pattern is very tailored, and it reaches clear to the floor. I am making it out of striped silk shantung.

Sewed all afternoon on my robe. Got it all done but the hand work. It was so easy and quick to do. It surely is a cute snappy looking affair. Met Ray in Jersey at six and we had supper at his house. Went to Lowe's and saw Jean Harlow in "Susy". Expect to go swimming tomorrow.

Ray came over tonight and we sat home and listened to the Sharkey - Lewis fight. Joe Louis knocked Sharkey out in the third round. I won 60 cents!

Betty, Ray and I went up to Dad's club today, Briar Hills Country Club, and had a lot of fun. Met Pops up there and we all went for a swim in the pool. There was a tea dance in the evening so we stayed for that and had dinner there. A nice day, but a terrible electric storm blew up tonight and we had to drive home through a regular flood.

Ray's cousin, Dick Kennedy, was visiting Ray for a few days, and went back to Notre Dame tonight. We went down to see him off on the midnight train. He certainly is a nice boy, 26 years old. He's studying to become a priest, and he only gets to come home to see his people every three years

Today is Labor Day and the whole weekend was perfect weather, so the summer wound up in grand style. Ray and I went to the science museum in Radio City this afternoon. It was so interesting that we spent 3 1/2 hours there. It was so wonderful having Ray home for a good long time, six weeks!

I had a nice relaxing day today and read a very good mystery story all evening, "The House that Jack Built ".

Made the cutest pillow today for a bedroom chair. A perky little ruffle around it, so feminine. Covered two sofa cushions, and the seat of the desk chair. I surely am tired. I've worked so hard the past two weeks. When we get moved, I'm going to bed for a week and rest up, and try to get rid of this terrible head cold that I have.

Mother started my sewing today. Ray and I expect to be married the end of next month so Mother is going to make me several nice dresses. I am sewing some underwear for myself. Satin slips and panties. Didn't go out all day. Ray brought me "Gone with the Wind", a very popular book that has everyone raving. It is a very interesting story about the Civil War days. I didn't get a chance to start it yet, but I will very soon.

Today is November 3, 1936, and this is election day. Roosevelt won over Landon. Ray and I went downtown and took part in all the excitement with the huge crowds.

I didn't see Ray tonight, so I worked on my new slip all day. I am on my second one now. They are so pretty, heavy satin with lace, and as pretty as any seven dollar or eight dollar slip that you'd buy.

Mother, Betts and I took a nice long drive this afternoon. It was so nice and sunny out. So far the weather has stayed very mild. I dread when it begins to snow and freeze. We all went out to see a movie tonight, but couldn't find one we hadn't all seen so we came home and made some fudge.

Ray's cousin Father Hart, who is going to marry us, is here in Boston. So we went to see him today; he was so surprised. He knew Ray was here, but he didn't expect to see me. He said he would come to Jersey any time to marry us, so we set January for our date. Father Richard was here too. He's a lot of fun.

Such a beautiful sunny Thanksgiving day. We had a 15 pound turkey and several couples came to join us. I'm so full of turkey I feel as if I never want to see food again.

Another rainy day, so I stayed in and sewed. Dad was home sick with a cold all day. The whole world has been watching the news the past few weeks over King Edward of England's wish to marry the American woman, Mrs. Wally Simpson. Parliament wouldn't allow it, because she was a divorcee, so the king abdicated, and gave up his throne and country in favor of this woman. His brother, the Duke of York, will succeed him as King George the VI.

King George with Queen Elizabeth

Had a nice big Sunday dinner at Ray's house. His whole family is excited over our wedding in January. We won't be able to set the exact day until Ray has a talk with his boss.

Ray and I met dad this afternoon and he took us to see Mr. Zaret, a friend of his, who is a jeweler. He had some wedding bands there for us, and I picked out a beauty. It is a platinum channel ring, set with diamonds all the way around. Mr. Zaret can save Ray about 50% on what he gets. I was so thrilled picking it out.

I met Ray downtown at Mr. Zaret's store at 7:30 and we looked at engagement rings. Ray's going to give it to me for Christmas. He got me such a beautiful one, a round diamond in a square, platinum setting, with three small diamonds on each side. I can hardly wait to get it in a couple days.

Ray and I went back to the jewelers today and left my ring to make it smaller. We came home and played bridge and then had a little midnight snack. Ray got my wedding band engraved and it says R.N. To E.W. '36.

New Year's Eve and the end of another diary. Ray and I went out to dinner with Mother and Dad, then we came home and had a few drinks. After that Ray and I went to a midnight movie. We didn't want to go out formal and spend a lot of money this year because Ray's going to need every cent when we get married next month. This ends 1936 and ny diary for this year.

1937.... Beginning a new year. Stayed at Ray's house last night. I'm so glad we didn't go out and celebrate a lot last night. We felt so good today and everyone else had hangovers. Ray and I drove over to Staten Island for a lovely day today.

Mr. and Mrs. Harry Beach Wheeler

announce the marriage of their daughter

Elinor Mary

to

Mr. Raymond Francis Nichols

on Wednesday, the twentieth of January

nineteen hundred and thirty-seven

Yonkers, New York

Ray and I had to go to church tonight. I have to go three times to get dispensation before we are married because I am not a Catholic and Ray is. The date is definitely set, January 20, at Saint Alden's church in Jersey and father Hart is coming down from Notre Dame to marry us. Ray and I are so excited.

We went to Jersey and picked up Ray's sister Angie, and we all went to City Hall to get our marriage license. It was such fun. Carl Feldman came over tonight and we all drove mama Nicks up to Patterson. It was such a terrific fog we couldn't see a foot in front of the car, but we made it safely.

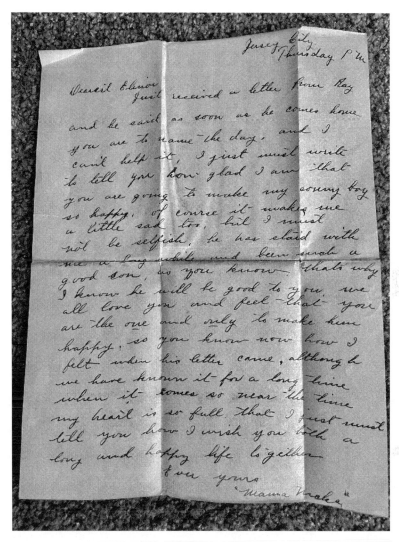

EDITOR'S NOTE: Precious letter from "Mama Nicks" to Elinor regarding Ray and Elinor's engagement.

Ray and I drove up to Paterson to bring Mama Nicks home and I got the biggest surprise of my life. They had all arranged a shower for me and I never had the least suspicion of it. It was the grandest thing that ever happened to me in my whole life. There were 25 people there and each one had a gift for me. It was a kitchen shower...dishes, and linens and things for the kitchen and everything was fixed up so lovely. Didn't get back to Ray's house till 4:00 AM. And 11 days, we will be married! In 11 days, I will be Mrs. Ray F Nichols!

Spent most of the day writing, thank you notes, and invitations to the wedding. Only nine more days, it's a week from Wednesday that we will be married.

Ray had to go out of town for a couple days on business. I surely miss him when he is not here with me. This time next week I'll be Mrs. Ray F Nichols!

Did some last-minute sewing today. We're going to have the reception here after Ray and I are married, so there is plenty to be done. Colored Eleanor is coming tomorrow and stay over until Wednesday night. She can clean the house good and help with the food. Ray came over for supper tonight, and is going to stay all night and go to the office in the morning.

Spent the day doing last minute things. Tomorrow is the big day, and I am so thrilled and excited. I can hardly stand it! So many beautiful wedding gifts have come.

January 20, 1937. Ray and I were married today, and I am the happiest person in the whole world. We had such a lovely wedding at Saint Alden's rectory in Jersey. Father Hart married us, and I think he was the most nervous person there. We had a nice reception at my house afterwards. It was snowing all day long and it was bad driving, but about 35 people came. It was such a bad night. Ray and I didn't want to drive too far, so we only came as far as Newark staying at the Robert Treat Hotel, and tomorrow night will go on to Washington.

Robert Treat Hotel. 1930's

Ray and I spent the whole day seeing Washington. Went through the mint, where they make money, through the buildings of the Smithsonian Institute, up in the Washington monument and saw the capital and the White House. Tomorrow will have to finish up what we didn't see you today. It is so warm here we can hardly stand our heavy coats.

We went to the dog races tonight with the Bermans, and we all wished that we had stayed at home. They lost $15 and we lost $10. We'll have to eat beans all next week.

What a grand day this was. There was a lovely big luncheon and bingo for the ladies at the convention this afternoon, and tonight was the banquet and formal dance. I was quite the belle of the ball. I surely had a lovely time and don't think I missed a single dance from the time it started at nine until the orchestra quit at 2 AM. I didn't win any of the door prizes, but they gave away a lot of lovely souvenirs.

Christmas day, 1937. My first Christmas as Ray's wife, and such a happy one. We came home from Jersey last night, or rather this morning, at 5 AM, so we could be here with Mother Christmas day. I got lovely gifts from the family, and we had such a grand big turkey dinner. We went back over to Ray's house tonight for another big party.

Ray, Mother and I drove up to Paterson today and Ray got a flat tire. He ran a spike of wood through a rear tire. He was so mad. Now we will have to spend $12 or $15 to buy a new tire!

December 31, 1937. This is been the grandest year of all, because I was married last January, and I have been so happy as Ray's wife. He is so sweet and good to me and everything is breaking just right for us. In less than a year after we were married, he got a grand new job for much more money, and such a wonderful territory all through the South. He starts in January so we will have a lovely winter where it's warmer. This is the end of 1937.

1938

EDITOR'S NOTE: Now that the Wheeler Twins vaudeville career is over, the diary entries are not as exciting. I have chosen the most interesting entries from the year 1938 and will share them now...

Miami at last. Got in about 3 PM and it is hot and crowded here. Ray has several days work here so we will stay over the weekend. I love it so, I wish I could stay a couple of months.

We stopped in and saw Bouche' at the Villa Venice in Miami today. Then we went up to the Deauville and saw Freddie Daw, he's married again. Tonight we had a grand time, got all dolled up and went to the Coral Gables Country Club, and saw Karl, who is manager there now. Betty used to be engaged to him.

Coral Gables Country Club. 1938

I had such a grand surprise today. Ray bought a grand big radio for the car, had it installed, and surprised me with it. It has the loveliest deepest tone, and not a bit of static, even over car tracks. It's the big $69.50 Chevrolet deluxe set, and he got it for $35 installed. It's a brand new 1937 set which they were selling out to make room for a 1938 shipment.

Ray and I saw "Snow White and the Seven Dwarfs" tonight. It is the new full length animated cartoon, all in color. It surely was good.

EDITOR'S NOTE: Walt Disney's Snow White and the Seven Dwarfs. Animated movie released in 1937. It was the first full length animated feature film.

Mother sent me the loveliest blue formal dress for Easter. It came about 5 PM, just in time, because Ray and I went out to the Coral Gables Country Club to a big dance, and to see Karl. I didn't have a long dress to wear, so I was just tickled to death when it came. Fits me perfectly.

In Columbus, Mississippi tonight. We ran into more rain just before we got here, and we skidded off a bad stretch of road into a deep ditch. We had to be towed out. It was a clay road, and the rain had made it just like quicksand. Couldn't control your car to save your life.

In Spartanburg, South Carolina tonight. We found a nice bunch of mail from home, and it made us feel so happy. The Louis/Snelling fight was tonight, Louis knocked Snelling out in the first round, two minutes and four seconds. Such excitement!

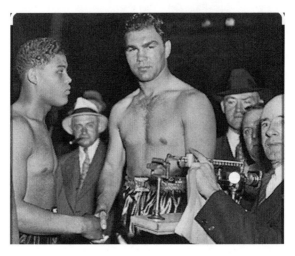

Joe Louis and Max Schmeling (1938)

EDITOR'S NOTE: Max Schmeling paid for Joe Louis's funeral in 1981 and was one of the pallbearers. Schmeling died at age 99.

Stayed in Orlando, Florida tonight. We stopped in to see the new Marine Studios just south of Saint Augustine. It was so interesting, all kinds of big ocean monsters, and tropical fish, and you look at them from underwater through glass windows!

In Miami, Florida again. Staying at the Norman Hotel this time on the beach. It's a beautiful place with a big garden patio and private bathing beach.

Had a grand time tonight. Went out to the Coral Gables Country Club. Freddie Daw is orchestra leader there now and is manager while Karl is away. Karl had to take his father up to New York to the medical center. They think he has cancer.

I had such a grand time tonight. Freddie and his orchestra were playing on the Everglades roof, so we went up there and danced, and when they finished, we went out to the club with Freddie while he checked out there and locked up. He certainly is a lot of fun. This is our last night in Miami.

Mother's birthday is September 2 so I thought I'd better do my shopping for her. I bought her a lovely little black dress, trimmed in white. She'll be needing it soon to travel home.

Saw the grandest movie tonight, Mickey Rooney in "Love Finds Andy Hardy." Mickey Rooney was younger than us, and he would often ask us to play jacks with him backstage before he went on with his family, and before we danced. He likes us a lot, maybe he has a cute crush on us.

Mickey Rooney in 1938

We stopped at a tobacco warehouse in Alabama today for awhile this afternoon and listened to them auctioning off tobacco in that funny scratchy throaty voice they use. It was so interesting.

We really needed a new car as we put so many miles on the car we have because Ray covers such a big territory in his work. We bought a beautiful Pontiac coupe today, deluxe, eight cylinder, dark gray with white sidewall tires. It surely is a beauty.

1938 Pontiac coupe

Of all the rotten luck! We landed in Spartanburg, South Carolina at noon, and thought we'd better take the new car into a Pontiac place as we kept noticing a grind in it. It turned out that it needs a whole new rear end, new shock absorbers, new clamp, and something done to the knee action and it won't be ready until three days from now. That's what you get for buying a new car too soon. We should have waited until around the first of the year until these new faults were corrected.

Well, they had to send our new car to the factory in Michigan for a new rear end and it hasn't come yet. Goodness knows how much longer we will have to wait for it.

The parts for the car finally came in late this afternoon. Hopefully we can now leave here about noon tomorrow.

The car was ready by 10 this morning so we finally got away from Spartanburg. We are in Atlanta, Georgia now for the weekend. Robert Fulton Hotel is where we will be staying. We're going to have Christmas cards made from some photos we had taken a few weeks ago. This will be so fun. Thankfully, the car runs like a dream now.

EDITOR'S NOTE: Photo on their first Christmas card sent out as a married couple, Mr. and Mrs. Ray F. Nichols.

Such a lovely Christmas today. We came back here to New York last night so we could have Christmas morning with the folks. We received some lovely gifts. I got a mix master, set of mixing bowls, and Ray gave me a beautiful knitting box filled with underwear, stockings, perfume, and two absolutely beautiful pins with my initials carved out. I love them so much. One is silver and one is gold and they are both studded with little diamonds. It's been a wonderful, wonderful Christmas and next month we will have been married for two years! I am a very happy Mrs. Ray, F Nichols!

EDITOR'S NOTE: Two beautiful pins I now have in my possession.

This is the end of 1938.

EDITOR'S NOTE: since the Wheeler Twins career has ended, and my mother and father are now married, I will add just a few more diary entries regarding their first born child's birth... Barbara, me! When you read this section, keep in mind, this was 1940, and childbirth and care for the new mother is totally different today... You may find these comments almost humorous as you read on...

May 17, 1940. This is the most surprising thing! I am in the hospital to have my baby. My water broke last night, and I phoned Dr. Seibold but no pain started. This was happening just as my bridge party was leaving. Luckily, Ray came home 30 minutes before. Here I am, starting in labor. Dr. S. said to bring me into the hospital so here I am. However, they don't expect the baby tonight.

Had pains all day, but far apart, and not very hard. The baby is not really due until June 14, but after examining me here at the hospital, Dr. S. says that we miscalculated the date and it's a full nine month pregnancy. Ray and I are so happy that it will be three weeks ahead of what we thought.

May 20, 1940 A 6 pound 2 1/2 ounce baby girl was born to us tonight at 8:32 PM.

I am up in the clouds with joy, and so is Ray. We're both so happy it's a girl and she's really lovely. She actually looks like Ray, has his dark hair and dimples and dark blue eyes. We're simply beside ourselves with happiness. Ray is simply beaming all over the place. Mother got in this afternoon from Indianapolis and was so surprised because of course the last she heard we expected the baby in about three weeks from now. We are going to name our baby Barbara.

EDITOR'S NOTE; This is extremely interesting how brand new mothers had to take care of themselves for an entire month after the babies birth!

May 27, 1940. After being in the hospital a week, I'm back home now and so glad to be here. I came home in an ambulance and have to stay in bed here for two more weeks. I have a practical nurse, Mrs. Lewis, to take care of me and baby Barbara and Mother is here of course so everything is fine. It is so nice to know that I will have the baby right here in the same room with me.

May 31, 1940, Dr. S. came to the house to see me today and said I was getting along fine. He left me a list of instructions for next week which will be my third week. I can gradually start doing a little something, exercises in bed, sitting on the edge of the bed and sitting in a chair for 1/2 hour. By the end of next week, I'll be strong enough to stay up.

*Mrs. Nichols*

## AFTER DELIVERY INSTRUCTIONS

### Dr. J. L. Seibold

**6/1/40** Knee chest posture twice daily—5 to 10 minutes—until baby is 6 weeks old.

Report if menstruation continues after you are up and around.

**6/3** → May sit on edge of bed with feet off on floor and exercise ankles and knees several times.

**6/4** *sit in chair ½ hr. 4 times*

**6/5** → Walk about bedroom if you feel all right; may go to bath room, living room, etc., later in day.

**6/6** — May take tub or shower bath, even if menstruating a little.

**6/7** → Take hot douche daily while in bath tub on your back; use one tablespoonful Boroaseptic Powder to ½ gallon warm water, even if menstruating a little.

Do not use stairsteps or go out of house until baby is 4 weeks old; may then go for ride, to movie, etc.

Do not shampoo hair until baby is 4 weeks old.

Do not drive car until baby is 5 weeks old.

Lie down and rest from 1 to 1½ hours each mid-A.M. and P.M., until baby is 6 weeks old.

Come to office when baby is 6 to 8 weeks old.

June 5, 1940 Sat in a chair a couple of times today, and it felt so good, but I certainly am weak. This is my third week in bed, and by sitting in a chair and walking a little bit every day, I'll have my strength back by the end of next week and should be able to stay up after next Sunday.

June 9, 1940 We took some pictures of the baby and I was in them too. I'm not supposed to go out for another week, but I just stepped outside the apartment door in my housecoat, so I could hold the baby and have her picture taken that way. We took a whole roll and I do hope that at least one of them is really good. Ray and I are so overjoyed with our new baby girl. We are going to love being parents!

EDITOR'S NOTE: To complete this book, I have posted several photos to honor my sweet mother's life.

Birmingham, Alabama.

First cold weather as a family of three...

Ray with his mother, Ellen Nichols, "Mama Nicks". Christmas, 1940.

"Mama Nicks" with her first grandchild.

EDITOR'S NOTE: My grandmother, Wilna Wheeler, the twins' mother, an incredible artist who painted for Hallmark cards made these two matching skirts with beautiful painted flowers on them for my mother and me.

1953. Ray, son Richard, Elinor, my Nana (twins' mother Wilna Wheeler), Betty, Freddie Daw, Barbara, Harry Wheeler, (twins' father

Elinor and Ray, my mom and dad, 1980's.

EDITOR'S NOTE: My parents were an extremely loving couple, held hands whenever they took walks, and loved to go ballroom dancing more than anything! They were always the center of attention of all the guests at the Coral Gables Country Club year after year, because of their outgoing personalities and their beautiful ability to ballroom dance!

My precious dad passed away at age 86 of cancer, and my mother had a rough couple years, but with love and support of all her family, she lived on her own happily, and energetically for 20 more years!

My mom's 95th birthday, 2005, shown with her two children, me and my brother Richard, who is five years my junior. I have three children, my brother, Richard has one daughter, so our mother was blessed with four grandchildren, and ten great grandchildren before her death at age 102.

2007, my mother at age 97 with her 10th great grandchild, Faira.

2007 magazine cover. My mother with her youngest great granddaughter, Faira... Still kicking her leg up!

My Christmas card in 2010, celebrating my mother's 100th birthday!

EDITOR'S FUN NOTE: Me with my two daughters, Cathy and Krista... They say that "the apple does not fall far from the tree"......,... Do you agree?

EDITOR'S NOTE: My mom, Mickie had quite a few "Mickieisms "as we love to call them. A couple of her favorite were "Jibby, Jibby" when she toasted with her glass when having cocktails, another of her favorite sayings was "My Irish luck!" whenever she found an up-close parking place, or anything else that fell into place with luck! Another...... if one of us dropped a little food or something on our clothing, especially while eating, she would immediately say "It will never show on a galloping horse on a dark night!". And her favorite of all sayings was....."And I started the whole thing! "talking about her children, grandkids, and great grandkids. Whenever I would ask my mother what was her very favorite time of her life, she would always say "Right now!". God bless you, Mickie, you are so loved! ♥♥♥😊

My son, Robby, gave me this gift of being able to write a book which I have done entirely on my iPhone! Robby and I read all the diaries out loud together and marked the pages that we felt were interesting enough to put into this book and then, in my own quiet time , I verbally dictated into my iPhone all the pages that we marked. Some of the entries are a day or two apart, and some are a month or two apart. But each paragraph is a different day. In addition to including many of the photos that I had of the Wheeler twins, I took the liberty to google other places of interest and famous people who touched my mother's life. I hope I did not overstep any boundaries by googling and printing anything without permission. I certainly did not intend to do that. I have spent over five months putting this book together, forgive me if it is less than perfect, but it was my very fun "do it yourself project", and I have enjoyed every minute of it. I hope my family and friends enjoy it as well.

I love you.
Barbara Nichols Kirk Patch. (Age 83)
June 2023.

Made in the USA
Columbia, SC
06 December 2023

27850183R00157